There Is a World
Elsewhere

Riverhead Books

A MEMBER OF
PENGUIN PUTNAM INC.
NEW YORK
1998

There Is a World Elsewhere

AUTOBIOGRAPHICAL PAGES

F. Gonzalez-Crussi, M.D.

Riverhead Books
a member of
Penguin Putnam Inc.
375 Hudson Street
New York, NY 10014

Library of Congress Cataloging-in-Publication Data

Gonzalez-Crussi, F.
There is a world elsewhere : autobiographical pages /
by F. Gonzalez-Crussi.
p.   cm.
ISBN 1-57322-117-1
1. Gonzalez-Crussi, F.   2. Pathologists—Mexico—Biography.
I. Title.
RB17.G66A3   1998
616.07′092—dc21
[B]   98-15520 CIP

Printed in the United States of America

1   3   5   7   9   10   8   6   4   2

This book is printed on acid-free paper. ∞

Book design by Amanda Dewey

Acknowledgments

Portions of this work were written in the Bellagio Center of the Rockefeller Foundation, by Lake Como, Italy. Having lodged me in a setting that Henry Wadsworth Longfellow once described as a "place of supreme and perfect beauty," the foundation in its generosity can take credit for any part that may be deemed comely, fit, or pleasing in this book. For its blots and imperfections, I alone must take the blame.

Contents

———

There Is a World
Elsewhere

Foreword

———

*A*utobiographical texts make notoriously treacherous grounds. Those who venture forth therein invariably lose their bearings. This is true at least in one respect, that authors in this genre profess to do one thing and end up doing another. Stendhal tells us (*Vie de Henry Brulard*) that he toyed with the idea of writing his memoirs for years. The first time this idea came upon him was on October 16, 1832. He remembered well, because that day he was about to become fifty years old. He wrote on the inner surface of his belt, "I am going to be fifty," in a peculiar cryptographic script, which only he could understand: *Jvaisa voirla5 (=Je vais avoir la cinquantaine).* And straightaway he said to himself: "I should write my life, and I shall know, when all this is over, in two or three years, what I have been, whether happy or sad, clever or stupid, brave or timorous, and, in the end, happy or sad. . . ."

To believe his words, he refrained from executing this

project out of modesty: "What an awful quantity of *I*'s! Enough to upset the most benevolent reader." He even thought of writing the book in the third person: *He did, he said*. But this approach was incompatible with a proper depiction of the most intimate motions of his psyche. And these perplexities stopped him from beginning his book, until November 23, 1835.

Now, any reader who picks up the book would never suspect that the author struggled three years against a modesty-inspired reticence to use the first person singular pronoun. Almost every aspect of his youth is described, in prolix nimiety, with Stendhal's facile verve. Childish drawings (this magnificent novelist showed himself an execrable draftsman) accompanying the text give the reader more topographic data than he or she might care to know. Floor plans of his house show where his bed was, where the window, and even where hung the cage with the family's parrot. In sum, Stendhal was far from the modest image he raised to his readers. He did not stop the outpouring torrents of *Je* and *moi* against which he had declaimed. And I doubt that he was any wiser for the writing, or more insightful of his own self at the end of it.

Jean-Jacques Rousseau incarnates the canonical literature of self-disclosure. This man tells us, in unexcelled, quasi-biblical accents, that he will appear before the Tribunal on the day of the Last Judgment with his autobiographical *Confessions* in hand and say to the judge: "Here is what I did, what I thought, what I was. I told the good and the bad with the same frankness. I did not silence the bad, did not add to the good, and if I chanced to use some indifferent ornament, it was only to fill a space left empty by my deficient memory."

But after the trumpet blast dies out, we realize that he did not tell us what he did, what he thought, and what he was.

Like other autobiographers, he thought one thing and said another, and often did still another. The touching sincerity that he extols so eloquently did not exist. He knew full well that he was being listened to. And he playacted. Magnificently, as usual. He acted the role of "confessee." So that where a sin was needed, he constructed one, for effect. And where a virtue was required, he produced one too—by retouching a fault, if necessary. All for the sake of literary effectiveness.

Loss of original intentions is the rule. H. G. Wells wrote his *Experiment in Autobiography* allegedly to get rid of the doldrums. He was in a phase of fatigue, anxious about the imminence of old age and infirmity, and wanting, as he put it, "to get these discontents clear because I have a feeling that as they become clear they will either cease from troubling me or become manageable and controllable." Writing as antidepressant therapy? But from the first line, his voluminous self-disclosure is a ringing, optimistic affirmation of his belief in the value of his own work. The kind of work that, by its very existence, rules out depression.

There is no point in multiplying the examples. The foregoing should be enough to justify my having promised the publisher one book and turned out another. I wished to interweave autobiography and physiology. My original intent was to interject, upon a background of personal history, biomedical concepts relevant to growth and development. I soon gave up. The two voices were too discordant. When one spoke, the other fell sullen and disgruntled from the interruption. I must postpone for another day my attempt to make them harmonize.

Instead of the anticipated hybrid, half personal history and half natural history, I came up with a narrative of people and places I have known. I did not do it for self-knowledge. Nor was I out to combat spleen. I do not pretend to understand fully my motivation, although it is reasonable to suppose that, like all autobiographers, I was actuated by curiosity and nostalgia. Curiosity impelled me to track down half-forgotten faces, long-departed hours, and semi-erased images of a golden prime. Nostalgia infused me with the hope that all was not lost that thrived during that wonderful stage; that many things survived unharmed and recognizable through the vicissitudes of changeful time; and that even the friends and loved ones whose death passed for certain in the outside world remained very much alive in the obscure depths of my inner, private world. To bring them back to the light, I said to myself, would be to find my lost youth.

Thus, this book is, above all, a personal document and a work of nostalgia. It was undertaken in the hope that feelings, images, and ideas that had fallen, soft as snow, upon my brain, would still be found there, sheltered from time's rude molestation after more than half a century.

Accordingly, the pages that follow are not an account of a professional life in academic medicine. Nor are they one more chronicle of the grueling years of postgraduate medical training. What the reader will find here are discontinuous, impressionistic renderings of some scenes from a man's life. This man happened to become a physician. However, I insist, the order of the priorities that guided the present writing at all times must not be confused: a man first, and a physician second.

F. GONZALEZ-CRUSSI
Chicago
1998

I

Of How I Was Once a Mere Glimmer in My Mother's Eyes

————

A sinister legend has it that the Roman emperor Nero, having killed his own mother, ordered that her body be opened, because he was curious to see "the place he had come from." There is a graphic representation of this unwholesome, terrible curiosity in a medieval book kept at the Bibliothèque Nationale, in Paris. The rendering, by an anonymous illuminator active in the year 1450, shows the body of Agrippina the Younger, Nero's mother, lying inert on the autopsy table. Her abdomen has been slit open; loops of intestine protrude through the incision. Two personages stand close by, anachronistically rigged out in medieval clothes. One is the emperor, who we are to suppose is prey to a morbid obsession disguised as anatomical-embryological curiosity, further complicated, according to the chroniclers of antiquity, by troubling elements of incestuous voyeurism. The other individual is the dissector, a humble personage who, knife still in hand, recedes toward the head of the table, so that the emperor can take the best observation post. And a wise move this is, for quite apart from protocol requiring that a dissector yield to his sovereign, giving a wide berth to the likes of Nero strikes us as the very essence of prudence.

Most likely, on that occasion, the emperor learned nothing. For the appearance of the uterus is generally disappointing. It is a muscular viscus, shaped roughly like an inverted cone that has been somewhat flattened in a front-to-back direction. The ancient Greeks compared it to a wineskin, more recent anatomists to a small gourd; and what is there, we may ask, in a zucchini to fill us with awe and reverential admiration? Or in a pumpkin to make it fit to launch an emperor's career? And then, its location is frankly depressing. For the uterus happens to be placed behind the urinary bladder and in front of the rectum—that is, between the repositories for urine and feces, respectively. This anatomical fact means little for most of us, but it clearly distressed the potentates of antiquity. Recall that ceremonies of "deification" used to be enacted, by which a ruler could officially proclaim himself *divus*, divine. Add to this that gods are supposed to be born in Elysium, amidst the delights of ambrosia, or, if their fate decreed a rougher beginning, in heroic and sublime surroundings. Think, then, of the lowliness of the womb's topography, and you will agree that there was sufficient cause for disappointment on Nero's part.

On the other hand, being forced by nature to be born in a dump, or, more precisely, surrounded by the body's filth, can work both ways: to the proud, as a reminder of the vacuity of their pretense; to the meek, as a vindication of their postnatal struggle. In other words, the haughty may be sobered by the thought, amply exploited in homiletics, that however exalted their present station, the beginning is the same for all men, "and is always little," as Bossuet once declaimed. But the meek and unassertive might draw comfort from reflecting that no matter how insignificant their present achievements may seem, they are always an improvement over their original lot, which consisted of lying snugly head down "*entre la merde et lou pis*," as accurately, though rather indecently, described by an ancient French proverb.

When it comes to reflecting on my own origins, I definitely rank with the latter group, namely the positive-thinking kind, the cohort habitually disposed to flattering self-deception. For I see nothing in my early antecedents that could be shown off with pride. I recall no valuable heirlooms, no marks of worldly triumph in the family, but everywhere the blows of poverty, the pangs of want, the fierce clawing of misery before which men reel, baffled and beaten; and therefore I believe the simple fact of our survival, of my own survival, must count as much as the wealth and high estate that others flaunt but did not themselves raise. For often the escutcheon conceitedly displayed was earned by dead ancestors with brilliant deeds and thereafter maintained with nothing but swank and fatuousness.

I say this prompted by reminiscences of my mother's cheerless stories of her own childhood. She was born in central Mexico, in the state of Guanajuato, to a peasant family. Life in rural Mexico, to the lower classes, has ever been one of toil and privation. It was to escape these harsh conditions that her widowed mother packed her scarce belongings, snuggled her baby in a *rebozo* against her back, as is the custom among Indian women, and, holding with one hand her son, just old enough to walk, and with the other her shabby suitcase, made for the capital of the nation. The time was most inauspicious. The odds never favor the uneducated and poor who leave the countryside for the lure of the big city, but that year—1913—and that month—February—were singularly unfavorable.

The whole country was convulsed in the murderous rage of the revolution, and as my mother, still a baby, entered the City of Mexico warmly pressed against the back of my grandmother, the bloody episode since known in Mexican history as *La Decena Trágica*, "The Ten Tragic Days," was about to unfold. As far as I know, my grandmother never was clear as to the causes of the murderous battle, or which factions were clashing. Nor did it much matter, since each day the revolution seemed more like a furious melee in which constantly shifting parties massacred each other, prompted more by passion than by ideology. But she would never forget the war's alarms, the screams, the terror of the population, the thunder of the cannon, the crackling of the rifle shots, and the moans of the wounded, prostrate and trampled in the dust, their wan faces streaked with crimson. And she obscurely remembered that in order to reach the address they were looking for, they were forced to contour streets and alleys where unnumbered dead sprawled on the ground, looking vacantly skyward with congealed, stony eyes that black birds were pecking. In the streets around her house, the *federales* and the men of General Félix Díaz, alike young boys and hardened soldiers, the gallant and the coward, found a common grave, all in a heap and emanating the same disgusting stench.

After the elitist oligarchy was toppled and Mexico became, at least in theory, a constitutional republic, things did not get much better for the dispossessed. Lacking the skills needed for survival in a big city, and at a time when all manner of social restrictions still weighed heavily upon women, my grandmother was forced to join the ranks of the urban proletariat. She had worked in the fields of Guanajuato; now she became

a worker in a factory of ceramic products, elegantly called El
Anfora (The Amphora). It was a family business, the property
of French entrepreneurs who somehow had managed to keep
the company going through the violent revolutionary period.
The owners, two brothers, disported themselves as *fin-de-siècle*
capitalists straight out of a "naturalistic" novel by Émile Zola.
And they looked the part: ruddy cheeks, long sideburns that
puffed round the jowls—so-called muttonchops—hair parted
in the middle, stiff starched collars, V-shaped beards à la
Mephistopheles, and luxuriant mustaches whose pointed tips
were carefully waxed and upturned with ad hoc little tweez-
ers brought from Paris. One brother was chief financial officer
and stayed mainly in the office, while the other, unable to sit
still, walked ceaselessly up and down the aisles, talked to the
workers, visited the furnaces, checked the enamels, supervised
the glazing process, and, at the end of the day, lingered around
the packaging area, where the working force was chiefly composed of young girls, a few of them pretty. Workers had few
benefits in those days, and bosses held a rather liberal concept
of the perquisites they themselves could claim; nor does it seem
that either of the two Duval brothers—for such was their surname—was above believing that sexual concessions were
more than incidental gains to which their privileged position
entitled them. This feudal mentality of the two bosses was especially apt to manifest itself when their respective wives were
not watching.

My grandmother was no longer young at the time. But although she was past her first bloom, she was still a vigorous
matron of supple waist, slender figure, and firm, sinewy limbs
that had something of the feline in their motions. Her raven-
black hair, which did not whiten until grand old age, was usually plaited into two long tresses that streamed loosely down

her back, ending in red riband bows; she wore ankle-high laced boots and long petticoats, which, fanning the air, seemed to stir a breeze redolent of the thistle and marjoram of her province, a breeze that could kindle unholy thoughts in one or the other of the Duval brothers—or in both at the same time. And she was a widow. And she was alone.

She was alone with the desperate loneliness of recent widowhood, dire poverty, lack of education, hostile social milieu, and two young mouths to feed. The mere evocation of her plight still gives me a shudder and a sense of anguished desolation. As my grandmother had to leave for work every day, and my mother was still a toddler, a means was devised to ensure the child's safety. A sort of harness with straps and strings fastened to the bed at one end and tied around the child's shoulders at the other, permitted her to move around the room but not to stray too far.

Thus, in my mother's earliest recollections—which, bless her heart, she has always retold with wonderful humor—she sees herself in some shanty, tied down to the bedstead. The roof is leaky, and the floor is the flattened bare earth. These deficiencies, however, are of little consequence. In the midst of all this squalor, golden sun rays stream through the window, brightening the soft, sweet air: for God, in his infinite wisdom, scourged the inhabitants of the Valley of Mexico with a thousand pains, and afflicted them with earthquakes and pestilence and discord, and made them pour forth salt tears, and then gave them in compensation balmy air and a sunny sky to enjoy almost all year round. Now and then, a chicken or a hen wanders through, cackling; the little girl is tempted to follow it around but is soon restrained by the straps. A neighbor drops in, to check that she is all right, perhaps to offer her some soup or to place a toy within her reach; for in those populous barrios of a time gone by, the sense of communal life was not much different from that in the village, and one could depend on the neighbors. At last, her brother would come back from school, and the toddler would be unstrapped.

Meanwhile, my grandmother endured the unsolicited attentions of a satyric employer, who could scarcely conceal his cloven hooves under shiny Parisian shoes with gaiters that buttoned on the sides. She might have given in, in due time; for chronic want and deprivation set a limit to everything, even a pious upbringing in the stern rules of the Holy Roman, Catholic, and Apostolic faith, as taught to young girls in the provinces of Mexico at the turn of the century. But it was appointed that her life would take a different turn. She worked at the potter's wheel. The wearing of protective apparel was considered a luxury. The spindle that supported her handiwork, gyrating very fast, caused the ejection of a bit of hardened clay, which struck her right eye. It was a catastrophe. The wound became infected, and the infection spread to the orbital tissues.

There she was, before the days of "workers' compensation," my unfortunate grandmother: in a rack of pain; in the blasting of fever; on a bed of affliction and sorrow. The wailing of her child, strapped to the bed's frame, could be heard now and then; as could the fluttering of the wings of the angel of death, who had come uninvited to sit by the bedside and stared at the patient with glowing red eyes full of a strange, sad eagerness.

The earliest distinct memories my mother has date from this period. She remembers that one late afternoon, a prim, dandyish Monsieur Duval appeared at the doorway. He came in without a word of welcome and sat in silence by the bedside. Of his reaction she has no clear recollection. Being no taller than the dining table at the time, she usually got a good view of the lower half of an adult body, but faces required the craning of her neck. Which is why she keeps a vivid memory of the man's shoes: they were in black, shiny patent leather and covered by gaiters that buttoned on the side. But she could not have seen an expression of dismay as he glimpsed the shabbiness of the ill-appointed room, the poverty and squalor of its furnishings, and, among the shadows, trembling, burning, tossing, my grandmother, her haggard face deformed by marked swelling and inflammation around one eye and moist with the sweat of anguish and illness on the brow.

The visitor did not stay long. He sat quietly for a few minutes, then hurried toward the door, as if, overwhelmed by the cluttered, oppressive atmosphere of the room, he had suddenly grown eager to plunge into the freshness of the vast and vacant expanse outside. Just as he was going to cross the threshold, he caught sight of the little girl. He approached her, bent down, and addressed her in heavily accented but kind phrases, then he placed a large silver coin of ten pesos—perhaps a week's wages—in her hand and rushed outside. The power of early impressions! To this day, about eighty years later, if she were asked to describe a Frenchman, she says, the first image to appear in her mind would be that of a tall, very tall man (the brothers Duval were doubtless both of indifferent stature, but to her that man had seemed enormously tall), so tall that one has to look straight up to see his face, in which the signal features are ruddy cheeks, auburn whiskers terminating in "muttonchops," and an upturned waxed mustache. Such a man is by nature benevolent—little does it matter that he may not indemnify a worker injured on the job in his establishment, or that he may take unfair advantage of his power to gratify his lust. The fact remains that he stoops down to talk to little girls;

and given the right conditions, he is likely to search into the pocket of his vest and extract therefrom a large, round, shiny silver coin, which he will proceed to press into your hand. A Frenchman, moreover, wears lustrous gaitered shoes.

Wondrous to recount, my grandmother recovered. The ministrations of the local doctor, and those of the *curandera*, combined their respective effects to set her back on her feet. Nor is it clear that the former were any more effective than the latter, at a time when antibiotics did not yet exist. In any event, she regained her health, although her vision was permanently impaired. The years that followed were not easy for her, since she had lost her job, but life went on. Realizing that life in a proletarian barrio exposes a growing girl to many more perils than she had foreseen or knew how to cope with, my grandmother eventually accepted an offer from relatives back in the province to house her little girl until she found a more secure employment. This is how my mother ended up back in the region known as Valle de Santiago, the state of Guanajuato, in the heart of the central Mexican plateau. Here, living with some distant cousins on a ranch, she passed her childhood years.

Those of us who were brought up in a big metropolis have some difficulty appreciating the unique charms of growing up in the countryside. Having known the squalor and destitution of poor neighborhoods in big cities, I am ready to concede that whatever disadvantages may be annexed to daily life on a ranch, these are likely to be preferable to the daily spectacle of crime, neuroticism, and moral misery that conform the landscape in the less favored areas of a big city. But this acquiescence of mine my mother deemed woefully insufficient. In other words, to say that life in the countryside is "likely" to be superior is not enough; nothing but the most vehement endorsement would do justice, in her opinion, to the real state of affairs. She had repined in the miserable human heaps that were rapidly growing around the City of Mexico; now the open spaces, the healthy air, and the beauty of the fields were to her a priceless blessing. Delivered directly from a humiliating bondage, a dismal situation that forced her mother to tie her down, literally, as one ties a pet dog, she could now stride happily in the meadows, in the company of girls her own age. I suspect there were negative aspects too. No place is without them. But to her eyes transfigured, her time on the ranch was as if spent in the Garden of Eden.

Eighty years later—almost a century!—her voice trembles with nostalgia when she reminisces about those jaunts across the fields that began early in the morning, after drinking milk, right by the milking stool, from earthen brown pots decorated by local craftsmen. The merry company of girls, laughing and joking, had their clothes drenched to the waist after traversing the fields of tall grass, heavy and damp with dew. They would pick, along the way, bouquets of flowers known in the region by evocative names: the collars of Saint Mary, the little bells of the bridesmaid, or the *cempazúchil*, of Indian appellation, and the yellow, fragrant flower of the huisache plant. They came back at lunchtime, to be served freshly made tortillas, fried beans with strips of a large green pimento pepper, a cheese that made long threads, and, on special occasions, tacos of *huitlacoche*, a true delicacy, a fungus that grows on the corncobs.

Hours passed away like minutes as they watched, lying on heaps of straw, the changing shapes of the clouds; or, deep in the fields, the restless bees among the shrubs; or, from the house, through the windowpanes, the farmers scattering the grain on the furrowed land. When it rained, how delightful it was to gather in the largest room of the house, listening to the clatter of the downpour on the roof tiles and to the tales of a wrinkled, bleary-eyed old aunt. She told stories that engaged the soul: of bloody feuds in the area, which passed down from generation to generation, like Sicilian *vendettas;* of ghosts and apparitions, like the hooded friars that were sometimes seen enveloped in mist, walking in procession through sombrous avenues of pines at the place called Cañada del Muerto, "Dead Man's Ravine," and were, she said, the blessed souls of purgatory; and many tales of banditry, of passion, of love, and of treachery and betrayal.

Each time my mother spoke of those years, the tone of her voice betrayed the fact that they had decked her life with color and excitement, as no other time had done, and therefore they became more and more idealized as they receded into the past. A light shone in her eyes each time she retold the same stories: the day when, walking down some sylvan path with her cousins, she discovered a beautiful, brightly colored ribbon lying on the ground and, as she stooped to pick it up, the alarmed screams of her companions made her realize that it was a *coralillo,* a banded coral-hued snake whose bite is often lethal; or the day when an older male cousin was kidnapped by revolutionists and had to be ransomed with piles of gold coins, which the uncle owner of the hacienda used to hide inside large, hollow leather belts worn around the waist and across the chest, like sashes; or the day when all the males were gone on business and the girls stayed up the night long, singing and laughing and telling stories, and one of them played the mandolin, and another disguised herself as a man and made the others double up with laughter as she entered the room clad in rancher's attire, pistol at the hip, huge sombrero on the head, and helicoidal mustache drawn with charcoal across her upper lip.

This bucolic bliss could not last indefinitely. The revolution had caused serious dislocations in all the strata of society. Banditry was rampant. With the breakdown of the established authorities, the countryside became unsafe. Commerce suffered. The cousins' ranch had to be sold. The family was fragmented, and my mother, though only thirteen years old, was compelled to return to the city to assist my grandmother in her difficult daily struggle. Thus her life turned again into a succession of dreary and toilsome routines. No more clover-scented breezes to refresh her from the rays of a hot sun. Vanished the cheerful tumult of laughing friends. She was back in one of those appallingly miserable shantytowns that surrounded Mexico City and still do so, in an ill-constructed dwelling that lacked the most elementary sanitary facilities. She washed clothes, prepared meals, shopped for food in the open market, and twice daily walked seven blocks to the nearest source of running water, down by José María Izazaga Street, carrying two large pails of water suspended with ropes from the ends of a wooden bar positioned across her shoulders.

Grim, indeed, are her reminiscences of that period which for most persons is one of sweet illusions, or of dreams high and fair. Her older brother returned from a day of harsh toil bad-humored, disillusioned, broken. His pushy, aggressive demands brought her back from her youthful fancies to an unforgiving, cruel reality. Years later, when she was asked if she had played with dolls as a child, her face grew somber, and her remembrance seemed to bring a mist before her eyes: she had owned one, and one only, a raggedy, rustic little doll given her as a Christmas gift on the ranch. She kept it as a memento of that most precious time. But one day, irked by her tardiness in preparing a meal and noting that instead of hastening to comply with his requests she dawdled and arranged the doll's dress, her brother fell into a fit of wrath, violently plucked the doll that she clasped in her hands, and threw it out the door into a gully. She never could find it.

I have often wondered what all this means. A little girl left alone, fettered to a bed inside an ill-outfitted room; an insensitive brother who, returning from the accustomed daily dose of toil, humiliation, and abasement, takes it out on his younger sister. The recitation of hardships, as I heard them, is in itself banal. Tales of privation and woe much more harrowing than these are commonplace in the crowded, poverty-ridden neighborhoods of any contemporary large city. If sometimes I try to examine these particular incidents in detail, it is only because they appear to concern me directly. If I fastidiously recreate in my imagination these scenes, which in themselves are trivial, neither exceptionally cruel nor unique in character, it is because I somehow feel that they were part of my coming into existence.

It is difficult to give a rational account of this feeling. Of course, I was not yet conceived. But the forces that draw a being into existence must surely begin to be activated before the first indications of its material existence. Causation is always manifold, as the schoolmen knew who spoke of efficient, formal, and material causes. And who can say that these ineffable forces, obscurely stirring in my mother's bosom, were alien to her childhood experiences? For to wrench from a girl's hands her only doll, as hers was wrenched, is to deny that make-believe maternity has any possible justification in the midst of societal violence and personal despair; it is to deny that playful illusion has a place in a world that closes down on us. To tie a child, as she was tied, is to deny that children are a bright promise for a better future; it is to say that today's need for survival supersedes any expectations of what is to come: for in a sense, there is no future. Harsh reality, which cuts down illusions, locks the wheel of time and cancels the future. But maternity affirms what these actions deny. Maternity is, in effect, all affirmation and optimism. By calling forth a new life, maternity peremptorily asserts that there *is* a future; that the end is nowhere near, and that all is about to begin. It says "yes" to futurity, to illusion, to love. Maternity and love course, both, in the direction of becoming. The stream of generation, of becoming, never stops; it flows onward without cease, while its counterpart, the flow of destruction, the river Acheron, as ancient poets named it, runs in the opposite direction. Thus maternity, like love, releases the locked wheel of time and promotes the actualization of numberless possibilities.

Still an adolescent, my mother married a man twenty years her senior, though by far the junior partner when it came to common sense. Marriage could have been a symbolic act of manumission, the rejection of the straps that tied her to a bed of want. And she conceived me, seven years later, under circumstances that I ignore. For all I know, conceiving me, too, could have been metaphoric: an act expressive of something else. I mean, drawing me out of nothingness might have had something to do with recovering her little doll from the gully into which it had been thrown. Of these matters I had no direct knowledge. I could not have had it, since I did not yet exist. And even after we exist, how soon can we know anything at all? In the Vedic literature of India, the *Gharba-Upanishad*, the "Upanishad of the Embryo," states that the fetus does not acquire consciousness until the fifth to sixth month of gestation. He, or she, can then know perfumes and flavors.

The ancient authors asked themselves odd questions about the unborn. Is the fetus awake or asleep inside the maternal womb? Is it animal or vegetable? Is the fetus an individual, or part of the mother's body? The Vedic text points out that after the fetus acquires spirit and consciousness—that is, after the fifth and sixth months of gestation—he, or she, can think. What of? An Indian fetus, if we are to believe the *Gharba-Veda*, shows a partiality for metaphysics: he thinks of the Imperishable and meditates on the syllable *Om*. In the ninth month, he remembers his previous births and has knowledge of his prior good and bad deeds. Shortly before coming out of the maternal uterus, he breaks forth in lyrical, inspired utterances: "I . . . have seen thousands of wombs before, and eaten diverse foods, and drunk from so many breasts! . . ."

According to this Eastern tradition, the fetus views the maternal womb as a prison and dreams of his delivery: "Alas! Plunged in a sea of grief, I see no remedy. If I am freed from the womb, I will take refuge in Mahesvara [one of the names of Siva], the one who ends all evil. . . ." To be born is to be freed from the womb, but to reach perfect peace is to be freed from all wombs, to break the chain that binds human beings to the ever-recurring cycle of reincarnations. A Western poet seemed to agree, who once declared: "I have been born, and once is enough."

I, then, was conceived, and developed tucked away inside the maternal womb: huddled, like all members of my species, in a not too distinguished enclave of my mother's pelvis. If I was able to distinguish odors and flavors as early as the Indian text says we do, I do not remember. Perhaps memory does not develop apace with sentience. Remembrance cannot stick to that soft jelly that makes up the immature human brain, needing a firmer substratum for a hold. Which is why the ancients believed it was impossible to remember things that occur to us before the disappearance of the "soft spots" of the skull. But although I have no memory of this, it is a safe bet that I did develop, and did so mostly with my limbs and torso curled up in a posture emblematic of total animal passivity and contented intimacy, the so-called fetal position. Thus I slumbered for months, still a stranger to tears and affliction. I rocked on the slight undulations of a watery environment, as we all rock, carefree and undisturbed, save for the echoing thump of a mother's heart, which says that God is in heaven and governs all the beings He has made.

And then one day—it was three o'clock in the afternoon, I have been told—the hand-to-hand combat was engaged: the struggle between mother and child, in which that one moans and grunts and sweats, and this one squirms to quit its cell, as a bird would escape from a snare. Neither of us knew why. Had I been able to ask my mother why did she bring me into existence, when so many good, solid reasons must have been apparent to her for denying me an entrance into this world, she would have answered: "I don't know. For no reason." Which would have been a way of saying: For the same reason that trees and plants grow out of the earth; for the same reason that I was brought here myself, with no one asking me: because the flow of generation, like that of love, is onward, ceaseless, unstoppable.

And so I left the womb and its primeval gloom, and emerged to the blaze of light outside, giving a loud wail. And as if by magical dispensation, straightaway I understood that the Hindus were wrong in calling the maternal womb a prison. It is man's first abode and finest shelter. Urged by life's cares, the weary and disconsolate often yearn to return thither. But it is too late. One does not return to the womb in the same way as the stray lamb returns to the fold. Only in dreams, or in death, is it granted to us to go back to the earth/flesh cavern. At the end of the journey we shall return to the ideal lee, the abiding shelter, our real country, our only true home. When all ends—the hope and the fear, the joy and the sorrow—only then shall we come at last to our own again.

The Box of
Distant Memories

———

I peer into my past as into a deep, dark well. Down at the bottom I descry something like a boiling in an obscure lake, an eddying mass of memories. I stand tense, keen, watching and listening, as a beast stalking its prey, my attention fixed on what was and is no more. Then the hoarded images reemerge. And I cannot help feeling astounded at the neatness of their features. They were buried so long, yet scarcely an erasure, a stain, or a rust spot mars their appearance. Hence the sense of witnessing a prodigy, like one of those consigned to hagiography, in which saints buried for years, then exhumed, were found to be miraculously preserved in fragrant freshness, with not a sign of corruption.

Thus it is that I can see again with meridian clarity the bedroom of my childhood. All its appurtenances are there: the brown metallic bedstead with recessed bookshelf space on its head panel; the nightstand with its lamp topped by a shade in beige cloth, the shade that was covered with red cellophane paper when I had the chicken pox, for it was common knowledge that red light shining upon pox-covered skin worked wonders to abate the attending misery; and the old-fashioned chiffonier against the wall, its double row of drawers separated by a mirror in the middle, and provided with rectangular heavy slabs of white marble for countertops. I can even see again, adhering to the lower left corner of the mirror, the sticker representing Mickey Mouse clad in the starry, oversized magician's robe that he wore in *Fantasia,* with a matching, conical hat whose tip appears bent and droopy. Mickey raises his large, chubby, four-fingered hands, conspicuously gloved in white, the indexes upturned in a gesture that may be taken for that of an orchestra conductor but which we knew—entire generations of children have known—to be the expression of unmitigated murine arrogance: he had usurped magical powers and went about practicing them to his rodent heart's content, just before being recalled to a humbler station by a blow on the backside from an irate Merlin.

All this I see with surprising clarity. It seems to me that one recalled image brings up another, and another, in its train. How this happens is one of the many mysteries we yearn to understand. Are memories like Epicurean atoms endowed with random motions, so that once stored in the box of the unconscious they must clash chaotically with each other and thus shoot out to the light of consciousness without rhyme or reason? Or are perceptions stored in orderly fashion like cards in an office file? Are we then apt to recall things that were contemporaneous with each other? Or are remembrances identified as preeminent under some other filing system, a unique attribution of value that may be termed the scoring system of the mind? To these questions there is as yet no satisfactory answer; but certain it is that as I evoke one image, a second one comes up, and then a third one, and then others of their own momentum, as if it were objectively true, and not purely metaphoric, to speak of memories as corporeal and mutually linked, intertwined, or spatially contiguous, so that where one is pulled out, the other must invariably follow.

So it is that I find myself again in my childhood's bedroom. It is on the second floor of a two-story building on a busy street. The contours of the furniture are visible in the prevailing semidarkness. The smell of the new fabric of the coverlets is perceptible in the air. A large window on the east wall looks directly to the street; its sashes are largely in glazed, rough-surfaced glass, painted white to dim the sun's glare, except at its center, where the windowpanes are made of smooth, utterly transparent glass cut out in the shape of a five-pointed star that becomes complete when the two casements are shut.

I find myself in bed, lying on my back and thus looking straight up at the ceiling. The exterior lights, cutting through the window, project a luminous image in the shape of a five-arm star. It is a pretty sight, of which I was formerly unaware. The beveled glass imparts an iridescent refulgence to the star's edges. The star of light materializes on my bedroom's ceiling in the early hours of the morning, when almost all the stores are closed and the conditions of illumination filtering in are just right. Otherwise, in the bright sunlight, or amidst the combined glow of car lights, streetlamps, and neon signs, the stelliform image is drowned and erased. But this time I can see it, because I am not asleep. It is two o'clock in the morning, and I have been awakened by a racket in the adjacent bedroom.

As far as I can figure it out, the boisterous commotion has this origin: my father, utterly drunk, insists on coming into my bedroom, to charge me with an errand; my mother is of contrary opinion and prevents him from entering.

"He is old enough to go," says he, with moderately slurred locution.

"He is only a child," says she, defiantly, "and he is asleep."

"He must go," he counters.

"He shall stay," she rejoins, inflexible.

Gradually, the situation becomes clear to me. The errand I am supposed to perform, if my father is to have his way, consists in going to the liquor store, one block away, to purchase for him a bottle of bourbon. For he falls prey, periodically, to this unquenchable thirst. It is an invincible, overwhelming, resistless force, under whose oppressive dominance he repines most dolefully. In vain has the family physician warned him that the liver, an organ indispensable to human life, is grievously injured with each binge. In vain did the parish priest adjure him, with solemn and eloquent entreaties, to quit a life of vice as perilous to his bodily health as to the chances of his soul's salvation. Useless were the admonitions of his brother, the supplications of his wife, and the stern reproofs of his mother, who now earnestly advised him, now begged him, to forswear a detestable habit that was, they all said, tantamount to suicide.

Now and then, intimidated by some warning sign, such as unusually severe pain; or affrighted by a terrible new symptom during a hangover, as when he was laid low by an episode of hiccups that lasted uninterrupted for three full days, and the doctor despaired of using inefficacious remedies, and his *compadre* spoke of having seen hiccuping victims who responded only to a brutal fist blow to the solar plexus; or filled with remorse after some shameful incident incurred under the daze of alcoholism; or overtaken with the sense of guilt upon considering, when sober, the suffering that he inflicted on his loved ones while inebriated . . . then, and only then, he would promise Our Lady of Guadalupe that he would reform, and light votive candles at her shrine, and make other conspicuous displays of his professed intent to turn a new leaf and embark on a route of undeviating moral regeneration. But all was in vain. Soon the unquenchable thirst would again clutch him and torment him, and his promises would be forgotten. This recidivism was witnessed so many times that in the end no one believed his protestations, nor did he care to renew them.

This time, the unquenchable thirst manifested with unaccustomed vigor. He had already downed six cans of Bohemia beer that he kept in the attic; exhausted what was left of the California wine contained in stubby, dark glass bottles lined up in the pantry; and searched through the reserve repositories and emergency hideouts known to himself only. And finding his supply utterly finished, he had thrown himself eagerly, frantically, upon a bottle of Yardley cologne, whose green liquid contents he imbibed in great drafts; and then turned to the Mennen aftershave lotion, whose alcoholic aroma seemed to him so inviting; and after this he rummaged through my mother's chest of drawers, opening bottles of lotions and perfumes, drinking each one in a single swill, only regretting that they should come in fancy containers so little capacious. And then he looked in the medicine cabinet, and he drank the cough syrup, which had an alcoholic base; and he turned next to the rubbing alcohol, and the ethylic ether, of which there was very little; and no doubt he would have imbibed antifreeze, or gasoline, or acetone, or paint thinner, had we kept any in the house, as the only sure way to quench the thirst once and for all—even if it meant putting out his life at the same time.

Then, staggering out of his room, enfeebled, seized by vertigo, and confused, but still thirsty, he hit upon the idea of sending me to the corner liquor store. At which time my mother planted herself firmly at my door, extended her arms across the threshold to bar him entrance, and resolutely held her ground. There was an exchange of words, then the noise of pushing and shoving. This commotion awakened me, and the first thing I saw was the luminous star projecting on the ceiling.

The remembrance now acquires a remarkable realism. I am lying in bed. Brought back from sleep by a sudden racket, as of bottles crashing, only gradually do I realize what is happening. Someone in the next room has just been pushed against a chest of drawers, and all the bottles and various objects lying on top have fallen to the floor. There follows a silent, tense effort, a dumb, relentless striving of two opponents: it resembles nothing so much as a wrestling match of a man and a woman. One wants to come in, the other impedes it. The man may have been the stronger, but in his present condition, spent, weakened, and more than slightly drunk, his strength is well matched by his opponent's.

Realizing who are the contenders, I am, at first, terrified and do nothing but stare at the luminous star above me. But, I hasten to add, it would be a gross inaccuracy to say that the scene is one of domestic violence: there are no blows, no direct intent to harm each other, no curses, no screams, no grinding of teeth, and no feeling of impending bloodshed. It is rather a tense contest of opposing wills and muscular strengths, a contest that I guess at but cannot see, taking place behind the door: I hear the subdued panting, the sudden dull shock of a back colliding with the door, and the muffled grunts of the two contestants as they struggle to unbalance each other or to gain an advantageous position.

How long did the struggle last? Not more than three or four minutes, which were for me as many centuries. I felt perplexed by a dilemma: should I come out or stay in bed? My first impulse was to get up in a hurry, come out of the room, and put an end to the deplorable scene. After all, I was, if not the cause of the conflict, certainly one of its essential elements. I felt it was well within my power to intervene decisively to modify the situation. I could always go to the corner store, I said to myself, which was a simple chore I could have accomplished in no time. On the other hand, I was only a young boy, six or seven years old, inured to obeying my parents, not to questioning their behavior or trying to impose my viewpoint on them. I also came to think later, but not then, that my mother attached a great moral significance to her resistance: a child should not be so used. However, some time elapsed before I realized that the struggle at my doorside partook more of the sports match than of destructive, criminal violence. I was immensely worried that more serious consequences might ensue. During this critical interval I did nothing. All I did was to stare at the luminous star, which displaced itself across the ceiling in concert with the passage of automobiles on the street outside. That is one fault for which I have never forgiven myself.

The lights of an approaching car shone against my window, and the incident light rays projected the star on a corner of the ceiling. In the general silence of the night, the increscent sound of an approaching motor coincided with a displacement of the luminous star: first slowly and obliquely, from right to left across the ceiling; then faster, as the noise of the oncoming car increased in pitch, according to the physical phenomenon that is known as the Doppler effect, and the onrushing car went by in front of the house. At the same time as the car coursed by, the star of light became elongated, as if

stretched, and disappeared in a far corner of the ceiling, only
to re-form immediately at its point of departure, waiting for
another car to set it in motion along the identical path. And I
stared, mesmerized, at this reiterative migration of the luminous star, while my father and mother, just beyond my door,
struggled with each other keenly, stubbornly, unyieldingly, not
unlike Jacob as he struggled with the angel.

I have since accused myself of connate cowardice, for not
springing to my feet immediately, to help my mother. A man's
mettle is soon apparent: other boys, at my age, would have
given proof of greater boldness. I stayed in bed, caught in a precocious form of Hamletian indecisiveness, watching a moving
star. That was the night I learned about shame. The scene perhaps prefigured my fate: to be caught unprepared, lacking the
nerve and quick mind that make for a man's success in the
world, and to remain ever neglectful of practical life for the
sake of contemplating the stars.

The father who so disgraced his own family life could
equally well disport himself with all the graceful dignity of a
loving and protective *pater familias*. Naturally. Why not? He
was a man, after all, and his behavior encompassed the astounding range of inner contradiction implied in a man's nature. After the thirst remitted, temporarily dissolved in spirits
of wine, his other, incorporeal spirits recovered their usual
buoyancy. After days or weeks of unshaven reclusion, of haggard withdrawal from all but the bottled obfuscation, he was
out in the world once more, carnation at the lapel, a charming smile on his lips and a multitude of farfetched, impracti-
cal, romantic, and ludicrous plans thronging in his brain.

He had been a distant father while I was an infant or a
very young child; but no sooner did I give proof of having entered the stage at which I might be presumed of attaining, as

it was said, "the use of reason" than he began to address me and generally to take notice of my existence. Never affectionately effusive, he showed an interest that was ostensibly genuine. It may be that sprightly, enthusiastic, and, to put it bluntly, immature natures such as his are never far away from the child.

It was during one of those periods of well-being that he found me playing in the patio with some friends and gave me a kaleidoscope. Such an impact it had! A kaleidoscope is one of the oldest toys, and surely it can be made to figure among the cheapest: nothing but a tube lined with mirrors at one end, where a few loose bits of colored glass have been placed; the observer's eye is applied at the other end, and what visual delight is obtained, what splendid optical geometry, what a unique, unforgettable phantasmagoria! A child never forgets the first time he gazes on that symmetrical, multicolored, shifting spectacle.

I can see myself, and my young friends, taking turns and eagerly vying with one another for one more peek, under the complaisant smile of my father. I remember discovering that the slightest movement of the hand caused a displacement of the colored bits of glass and a corresponding change of the pattern. The game then consisted, for me, in trying to turn the tube ever so slowly, to see how far I could rotate it before the image would shift. It was impossible to turn it around its greater axis more than a few degrees without causing an abrupt shift of the spectacle.

In the end, I did what every boy is naturally tempted to do with a kaleidoscope: I busted it. I forced open the bottom, to learn the secret of the marvelous sights. I counted the colored bits of glass enclosed therein; and I attempted to determine the placement of the mirrors, but their original position was irretrievably lost by the damage I had caused.

Try as we might, there is no repairing the disarray caused by our exploratory curiosity. For I am not alone in wreaking this havoc: Leonardo and his brother Moisés (Moses), my friends and neighbors, are with me. We introduce all sorts of objects into the kaleidoscope tube: a small leaf from a potted plant, grains of sand, fragments of a green-and-white-striped candy, and even a live ladybug. Alas, these objects, placed inside the bottom of the tube and observed from the other end, look exactly the same as when they were outside. Careful manipulation of the mirrors succeeds in making the images double; but the wonderful, symmetrical, shifting, multicolored reproduction of images is no longer possible: the charm is gone forever.

I try to remember other tracts of my childhood, but my effort is unsuccessful. I barely manage to re-create measly fractions of it. It bothers me that memory should be so patchy. I can see certain scenes with impressive vividness and exquisite detail; others are altogether blurred. In either case, I cannot recollect what preceded or what followed. It is as if I could discern little islands of light in an ocean of darkness. How come, I ask myself, huge blocks of time have managed to vanish from consciousness, leaving absolutely no trace? Bergson wrote somewhere that we marvel at our power to remember, when there is, in fact, greater cause to wonder how we can forget. He was probably right in believing that *all* our perceptions remain indefinitely; that our whole history is somehow contained in the mind, compressed inside it, waiting for the right stimulus to unfold it into consciousness again; proof of this is that those condemned to hang, or to the firing squad, or who in other ways believe they are about to die, claim they see their whole personal histories rolling before them, as in a fast-moving film. But now, endeavoring to remember my early years, I am simply amazed at the nearly complete loss. What did I do all those years? They left no trace. Yet I must have lived, since I am here now.

And of those things I remember, the detail is preserved, but the continuity is lost. A scene appears before me here, and another one there. Which took place first and which later? I cannot tell. I must resign myself to reconstructing isolated episodes instead of a continuous narrative. Only what good is that? It is like turning on the television when the program is halfway through, or turning it on at the beginning but switching it off at the first commercial, before the end. One sees the beginning only, or only the end; the episode loses all meaning. But this, it seems, is precisely the way I must look at my childhood.

In one scene, for instance, I see myself at a picnic, in a magnificiently wooded park, with my mother, my three close friends, their parents, and other adult persons. My father, of course, is not there: his sober intervals, rarer as time goes by, he uses to spin wild dreams and fantastic schemes that call him away from Sunday outings. My mother does her best to restore some steadiness to our household but must do this from a *de facto* widowhood, soon to become the real thing. All of which renders our destituteness more apparent: it is plain to me that my neighbors and friends have parents who are diligent, serious, and affectionate. And the fathers, I cannot help noticing, are abstemious to a fault.

Who are these picnickers? The adults, with the sole exception of my mother, are Jewish immigrants, an unlikely company in a populous barrio of Mexico City. But this, in fact, is our company. Their children became my close friends and assiduous companions throughout my growing years. In the barrio where we live they are widely referred to as *los rusos*, even though they never set foot in Russia. They came from Poland. How did they end up in Mexico?

Having become an immigrant myself, I have read with interest what some experts say about the determinants of migration. In general, their pronouncements have to do with pressures that drive out, and forces that attract, those who move from country to country. In the United States, the country of immigrants *par excellence*, the indrawing forces—that is, the factors that attract migrants—are often the subject of a disproportionate, prolix attention. For emphasis on the centripetal force is flattering to the receiving end: clearly, the reasons why a large number of persons choose to come boil down to the fact that the country is a desirable place of residence, a place in which many would fain spend their lives. It is a legitimate source of pride for Americans that the poor, the oppressed, the "huddled masses yearning to breathe free," should flock to America's borders. But it is not to be deemed cynical or insensitive to acknowledge that the forces that drive people out of their native countries are often far more important, in the immigrant's estimation, than the qualities—be they ever so excellent—of the land of promise. For it is rare for a grown-up person to leave his or her country willingly, without strong cause. One does not abandon family, friends, language, customs, and traditions without a major compelling reason. These are the stalwart supports of personal identity. A man does not sweepingly break away from all this, unless forced by extraordinary circumstances. The Jewish immigrants to the American continent at the start of the Second World War illustrate very clearly the higher relative magnitude of the ejecting forces. Getting out was a matter of sheer survival; where to, an altogether subordinate question.

It was definitely so in the case of my friends' parents. I

never was certain as to where, exactly, they were from. I once asked, and was told, but was too young for the name to mean anything to me then and have since forgotten. Lublin? Krakow? Warsaw? Czestochowa, Piotrkow, or some lost little village of unpronounceable name? It does not matter; what is certain is that they started off from some *shtetl* in a country where the winters were dark, cold, and dreary, but by no means as cruel as the pogroms—which were also endemic there, though less predictable. Then the Old Continent went mad. The cultured nations of Europe, in which anti-Semitism had been a subtle, constant presence, like a chronic illness tolerated on account of its low intensity and because it made a handy excuse for various follies of the body politic, suddenly relapsed into a feverish, convulsive, rabid hatred. There was strident propaganda, and *Kristallnacht*, and mass media diffusing inflammatory, hateful messages. All of which, though it now seems incredible, was a mere prologue to mass exterminations. Still more incredible, the social and political forces that might have been expected to rise in outrage to defend the victims did nothing. This was the attitude of Europe, cultured Europe, some of whose thinkers now marshaled "scientific" theories to justify the most horrid crimes. Many understood. Those who could got out. Among them were my friends' parents.

They were headed, like hundreds of thousands of their coreligionists at the time, toward the United States of America. But not all could be admitted here. There were bureaucracies to contend with, and forms to fill, and examinations to pass. A suspicious lung shadow on an X-ray film, a low educational level, lack of connections and influence in the country of destination: these were things that could have disqualified an applicant; and the door would have been shut before such a one, even when closing the door was the same as sending him to his death. For whatever reason, English-speaking North America would not have him. Then an officer came in and announced: Mexico would. And so it was off again, from Ellis Island, due south this time.

On shipboard, and only days before landing, a sailor sold my friends' father a Spanish-language textbook. This was his first conscious move toward becoming familiar with a heretofore utterly alien culture, in which fate had decreed that he should spend the rest of his life. I saw the book, for it was kept in my friends' house as a memento of those harried days. I cannot refrain from smiling, as I recollect the lessons in its pages. It was an old edition, printed I know not where, displaying the German equivalents, in Gothic characters, of the Spanish phrases. Ink illustrations represented guitar-toting, caped Spanish *caballeros*, large kerchiefs knotted around their heads, and arrayed in short jackets, with broad silken belts around the waist. They were shown speaking to dark-eyed young ladies clad in low-collared blouses that left their shoulders bare, unless covered by *mantillas* or shawls—women who sported carnations in their hair and wore ornately carved, massive combs for their headdress.

Interestingly, the student was shown examples of *piropos*, gallant phrases that, in Latin countries, men may say to passing beauties. But these expressions sounded so outmoded, and so exuberant and baroque, as to seem pillaged from Luis de Góngora, a Spanish poet of the seventeenth century, famous for his excessively convoluted style. And apart from the outdated Castilian and the intricate style, absolutely nothing recommended this textbook to the attention of an immigrant planning to settle in post-revolutionary Mexico. "*Adiós, serrana* [a specifically Spanish term for 'mountain girl,' also said of one of shapely body], light of my life," one could read in Lesson Six.

"Let the two refulgent stars that you have for eyes, brighter than the jewels of the Virgin's mantle, shine upon me, that I may go on living." It is highly doubtful that a Yiddish-and-Polish-speaking Jew, just out of the *shtetl* and disembarking in the sultry, muggy climate of the port of Veracruz, might have had occasion to use this and cognate expressions in the textbook, even if he had learned them by heart.

Indeed, the Spanish language proved to be formidably difficult for the immigrant couple. Long after they had fully integrated in Mexican society—he, whose name was Nathan, became *el señor Natán;* she, Klara, was to her friends *Clarita,* in accordance with that quaint Mexican partiality for the diminutive—they could not overcome a thick guttural inflection, clipped phraseology, and the systematic avoidance of the subjunctive and all complex verbal conjugations. These limitations must have tickled the fancy of a neighbor, who declared them "Russian." The label caught on, as preferable to Polish, Latvian, Estonian, or Lithuanian—species, these latter, whose very existence was unknown in the barrio. Hence my friends' parents became *los rusos*, without further ado.

Their struggle in their new country, though rich in incident, was essentially no different from that of immigrants everywhere. Señor Natán bought a gasoline station, just as President Cárdenas was about to expropriate the oil from foreign owners. Nathan had to start anew, from scratch. Later, after much toil, he acquired a modest hardware store. For this, the couple rented space in a modest building owned by my father. They were our first tenants. Then, years later, by unflagging effort, systematic economy, a frugal life, and long-sustained, honest work, they managed to set a little money aside. With a cautious attitude and a conservative outlook, in a country with a weak economy, there was no question of amassing a fortune. But their unwavering tenacity and orderly life led, in the end, to financial self-sufficiency. The children received a higher education, and there was no need to be subservient to anyone. They did not have to depend on others for survival.

All this contrasted painfully with my father's wild ways. He dreamed of instant riches, in the pursuit of which he struck odd associations and surrounded himself with eccentric characters, like escapees from a farce. Some turned out to be swindlers, and he the lamb they fleeced shamelessly. His own estate, not very large to begin with, was largely consumed in farfetched ventures. One of them was investments in the movie industry. While this fancy lasted, he used to come home accompanied by would-be directors, cameramen, and producers, or arm in arm with "starlets" or fancy women of show business, to the undisguised displeasure of my mother. One producer ran away with both the money and the leading actress.

My father's last venture was in mining. He knew nothing about mines but lived as if perennially hypnotized by the fabulous riches he had seen extracted from the earth in his youth. He bought an abandoned old mine near his hometown. It had long been exhausted. In its shafts were sunk the last residues of our patrimony, as he directed the excavations from a distance, much of the time through an alcoholic fog.

A man forced to emigrate behaves very differently. He seeks stability, not adventure. He has had enough of commotion and turbulence: it was some form of trepidation that shook him loose in the first place. All he wants now is a secure lee, a refuge from the storm. My friends' parents found it in, of all places, a proletarian neighborhood in the City of Mexico. Social services left a lot to be desired; but nowhere was there thought of constituting a hostile organization, an *Einsatzgruppe* in charge of destroying them. The natives were very different:

a volatile people, not sold on the regenerative powers of work; hard to understand but on the whole not unfriendly. They could evince fanaticism and ultranationalism—which people do not?—but did so rarely; and their xenophobia was usually of a coarse, relatively manageable kind. In other words, there was no high-flown talk of a grandiose racial community, no lofty-minded concept of a *Volksgemeinschaft*; therefore, no danger of being specifically marked out for exclusion as inferior-blooded.

It was the third world they had come to: an ugly world, mangled by poverty, disfigured by terrible social injustices. But here no one ordered them to live in ghettos, as they did in Warsaw, Bialystok, or Vilnius. They were not forbidden to walk in the parks, to go wherever they wanted, to attend the universities, or even to participate in local government if they felt so inclined. Here they could engage in any business or profession. They could intermarry, if they chose to do so. And to top it all, the weather was simply glorious almost all the year round.

Every time I think of it, I conclude that my friends' parents did not have it too bad, after all, in their transmigration. Yet like all persons uprooted and transplanted, they must have felt sad. There is a special kind of sadness, known only to migrants, that consists in never feeling quite at home. It originates not so much from looking different, speaking with an accent, or being dubbed "*ruso*" by Mexicans, "dago" by Americans, or "foreign devil" by Chinese. It arises rather from the realization that the very concept of "home" is illusory, like much of what passes for real. It springs from finding out, for instance, that the idea of "home" is made in equal proportion of warm feelings of familiarity and of exclusionary invidiousness; that the same sentiment that roots for one party reviles the others; that one never feels so much "at home" as when assured that no foreigners are admitted. Thus, to the migrant, home is nowhere. It is not the place he comes into: that is already taken; that is the rightful home of others. And it is not the place he comes from: that is already changed. Always. Above all, the migrant who was once driven out must never make the mistake of retracing his steps and going back after many years. He will find, in the place of a familiar garden, an expressway or a parking lot; the ancestral home bulldozed away, or bombed during a war, or, if still standing, inhabited by others (for "the same" invariably turn, with time, into "others"), or haunted by ghosts, or tenanted by shadows.

III

On Growing Pains, Acute and Chronic

———

$\mathcal{M}$y early childhood passed in relative financial ease. Before my father utterly consumed the family estate in the pursuit of his fantastic dreams, he hit upon a string of successful business ventures. These catapulted him higher and higher in his world of unrealities, toward a pinnacle whence, shortly thereafter, he was to drop precipitously to a ruinous end. But in the meantime there was an interval of tranquillity. We were modestly comfortable, and in the barrio we could be said to be well off. Direct proof of this was our ownership of the small building we lived in, with two apartments to rent; indirect proof, the resentment I read in the eyes of my companions and playmates. For annoyance at the good fortune of our peers may be uncharitable, base, and contrary to Christian precepts, but it is surely among the earliest emotions that shape in the hearts and minds of men. I was lucky. I was pampered. I was

lovingly cared for. Therefore, I was envied, resented, and sometimes made the target of hostile intent.

Not so with my neighbors next door, the three boys of the
immigrant Jewish couple. Whether because I was too small and
inconspicuous to be a real nuisance; or because I was, after all,
the son of the landlord; or on account of my mother's having
developed a genuine friendship with Clarita, the boys' mother;
or owing to a combination of all these, the fact is that I was
admitted to the neighbors' living quarters with unrestricted
freedom. Truly, I came and went as one of the family. I was apt
to be found in their place morning, afternoon, or evening.

I was, if I may say so, a sort of adopted little "goy" in their
midst. I was in their living room even as the *shofar* was blown
in the temple; lingered in the apartment during Rosh
Hashanah; hung around with my three friends on many a Sab-
bath; and do not remember being excluded from their company until, having grown old enough to realize the importance
and solemnity of the highest of holy days, I was tactfully made
aware that Yom Kippur is the time set aside for each man to
wrestle with his conscience, the Day of Atonement being best
observed in quiet prayer and undisturbed supplication.

By then I had become quite accustomed to the radio programs that the Ashkenazi community broadcast every Sunday,
full of catchy, lively songs in Yiddish that were rhythmically
punctuated by high notes of the clarinet. The words I could
not understand, but the plaintive inflections, the surging
laments of rapidly mounting pitch, the dragging notes reminiscent of flamenco, have tarried in my memory for more than
half a century.

In like manner, my taste buds became habituated to the
morsels that Señora Clarita doled out indiscriminately to her
offspring and me. Gefilte fish was uncommon, as it was not eas-

ily available everywhere in Mexico City at the time. Strange
as it may seem, the neutral, paperish or cardboard-like taste of
the unleavened *matzos* that we got at Passover I somehow
found agreeable, grew fond of, and in the end came to miss.
Such is the power of early impressions. Jewish authors have
tried to analyze the lasting effect produced on them by the syn-
agogue services on the high and holy "Days of Awe." To the
ecstatic recital of the reader, the sense of fervorous community,
the spectacle of congregants enwrapped in *talliths* or prayer
shawls and engrossed in prayer, one must surely add the young
age of the witness. There is an age when impressions settle easily into permanence, like deep prints in fresh cement. Over
fifty years later, I have surprised myself looking for a white
cardboard box with blue Hebrew characters, the box of *matzos* that I used to know, along the aisles of a supermarket. Many
brands now exist, and as many variants as unorthodoxy could
come up with. But nothing compares with the early experience I had of them, when I was the little Gentile appendage
of a warm and generous Jewish family.

However, the inescapable reality was that I had not been
born a Jew. Lest I should come to question my own identity,
limits had to be imposed upon my frequentation of the neighbors' home. My three friends ended up going to the Tarbut
Hebrew School, and I elsewhere. Our parting company at this
time was unfortunate, and I am sure to the detriment of my
education. For the preoccupation of Jewish communities with
sound academic achievement is proverbial. It is therefore likely
that all the schools that served that community, including the
one my friends attended, were quite good. My lot was different. To satisfy my father's vanity and my mother's earnest,
though ill-advised, desire to see me become polished and well-
bred, I was sent to a snobbish school, all artifice and pretense,

which bore the high-sounding name of The English School for Boys. This establishment had all the trappings of a British boarding school and none of its strengths.

It was not a boarding school, in the first place. Promotional brochures boasted of a commitment to the classical ideal of *mens sana in corpore sano*, but I saw little evidence that the school's resources were put behind this noble professed ideal. There was a tennis court, but neither trainers nor equipment; a swimming pool, which was always empty; and a library, for whose real existence I could not vouch, since it was perennially closed. However, the principal—*el señor director*, as he was referred to—was no doubt a very astute man who knew well how to impress the *nouveaux riches* who formed the bulk of his clientele. His office was all buckram and affectation. In it were gathered all the stagy, ostentatious objects, and all the humbug decor, that guile could think of assembling to inspire visitors with awe.

My mother and I entered the school, hand in hand, to register me for classes. The light was dim, despite the blazing Mexican sun outside. Darkness came from the varnished mahogany sideboards and the somber wainscoting of the walls. A collected atmosphere of almost religious character resulted from the semiobscurity, the muffling of sounds, the thick carpets, the high ceiling, and, to top it all, a stained-glass window, as in a cathedral. Its motif was a scene of British mythology or folklore, I could not tell which. All I remember distinctly is that it was rendered in a style that I later learned to associate with the Pre-Raphaelite painters. But the most remarkable sight was by the door, against the wainscoted wall, redolent of fine-grade wood: it was a black figure in a full suit of armor.

In effect, authentic armor four or five centuries old, or a perfect imitation thereof, stood by, like a sentry on watch. I had never seen such a thing, except in films and book illustrations. And here was this imposing, warlike figure, able to set on fire the imagination of any boy, complete with helmet, movable visor, embossed pallettes, a shiny breastplate, and iron gauntlets with spiked knuckles, which clutched a massive two-handed sword. I would have paid twice my week's allowance to be permitted to inspect it at close range. But the armor was kept in the school's *sanctum sanctorum*, to which children were never admitted, except briefly on the day they registered, in the company of their parents.

In retrospect, I realize all these were carefully calculated externals aimed at creating an atmosphere evocative of an exclusive English club, or the vestry of an ancient Anglican church where instruction is imparted amidst green lawns and moss-covered walls. Here, behind a massive desk on which stood a lamp identical to that which newspaper photos showed in Winston Churchill's office, sat *el señor director.* Although his surname was Spanish, his ersatz Britishness had become for him a profitable way of life. Consequently, he pushed it to a ridiculous extreme. In the sun-drenched climate that we enjoyed, he was rarely without his umbrella. Under the blue sky, with palm trees growing outside his office, he sported bowler hat and heavy tweeds. And in the summer, when we, the students, felt uncomfortable in our blue uniform sweater with its embroidered school insignia displaying the British lion, he would be seen gadding about in light-colored vest and jacket, a flat-topped short-visored cap, and trousers tucked under his socks, as golfers were wont to wear.

It was commonly bruited that often he went golfing, and this detail, at a time when golf was a sport largely restricted to the upper crust, enhanced the swank that so impressed the snobs who patronized his establishment. But it is interesting to reflect that the deceit and falsehood that trick adults do not always hoodwink children; often, these are wiser than given credit for. So it is that one day I saw our illustrious leader walking by briskly in his golfing attire, and somewhat intrigued by the unaccustomed clothing—for this was, in effect, unusual in the country and wholly unseen in my barrio—I naively inquired of a third grader who was close by: "Does he dress like that to play golf?" His answer was, coming from a nine-year-old boy, shocking in its cynicism and earthiness, truly worthy of a ragamuffin in a picaresque novel, and of a linguistic turn that I can only imperfectly translate. "No," he said. "He dresses like that because he is a fool with a liking for fart-trapping breeches"—*pantaloncitos de "guárdame-los-pedos."*

Other figures of that learning establishment cut a sorry figure in my memory. Among them is Mr. Saavedra, my third-grade teacher: a tall, lean, dry, gaunt man, of olive-tinted complexion, who wore circular metal-rimmed spectacles and dark three-piece suits, lustrous at all pressure sites from prolonged wear. He embodied the figure of the school *domine* of ancient times. Ill-fed, poorly paid, conscious of his social relegation, yet forced to kowtow to the principal and other school authorities, not to mention many of his pupils' parents, Mr. Saavedra was more than well disposed to vent his frustrations by abusing his students. His desk was by the window, at the head of the classroom, and so placed that in the morning, when he moved his head a certain way, his spectacles caught the incident light rays and sent forth sudden gleams, like flashes of lightning. This detail added an extra measure of effect to his intimidating, stern image.

I see myself in his class. The teacher has just announced that he is going to find out who knows the assigned lesson. We are supposed to have learned a short textbook chapter. There was no stipulation that we should learn the lesson by heart. "You can say it in your own words," we were told. But most of us find it very difficult to rephrase concepts we have read. How does one say "Vitamins are substances essential for normal growth" in one's own words?

The teacher grabs the roster and calls out my name. I stand up by my bench. "Do you know the lesson?" he asks. There is a newspaper on his desk, and without waiting for my answer, he takes it, opens it, and begins reading the headlines.

"Well?" he says, looking at me without lifting his head from the newspaper, raising his myopic eyes above his glasses, which hang midway down his nose.

"Vitamins are substances essential for normal growth," say I, gallantly venturing forth, and I continue thus: "Vitamin A exists in the livers of animals. It is essential for vision, reproduction, and maintenance of mucous membranes. Vitamin B6 is found in meat, yeast, seeds, and bran. . . ."

Here I stop. After a long pause, which seems not to disturb the teacher, I repeat: "Vitamin B6 is found in meat, yeast, seeds, and bran. . . ."

A second pause. The teacher stops reading the newspaper, looks at me, asks, "Yes?" and I repeat for the third time:

"Vitamin B6 is found in meat, yeast, seeds, and bran. . . ."

"You don't know," says the teacher, adding: "This will get into your report card," while he scribbles something with his fountain pen.

Then an assistant comes into the classroom to tell Mr. Saavedra that he is needed in the principal's office. The class is left temporarily unattended. There follows a wondrous transfiguration. The quiet, collected demeanor changes to one of excited deliverance. The collective attitude was one of submissiveness only a minute earlier. It is now replaced by a rowdy, boisterous expansiveness. The new mood is expressed by several possible gestures, among which individual pupils choose the one they prefer: to perform a war dance atop one's bench, while howling savagely; to throw bits of compressed paper across the room; to push one's enemies to the ground, swipe their lunches, or somehow harass them unawares; to dart blithely between benches, fast as squirrels, in pursuit of someone, to elude angered pursuers, or for the sheer pleasure of feeling oneself free and unconstrained.

On another occasion, late in the year, I see myself on my bench, anxiously worrying as the roster is being read. It is Monday morning, and we are expected to place our weekly report card, duly signed over the weekend by one of our parents, on the teacher's desk, one by one, as each name is called out. The fearsome Saavedra would not dispense with this opportunity to administer the rod to delinquents, regardless of their alleged extenuations. Therefore, delinquencies are few. As names keep being called out in strict alphabetical order, the pile of report cards on the teacher's desk grows taller. But I cannot find my own report card. I am sure I placed it in my satchel, but it is nowhere in sight. And the roster call advances inexorably.

I have never been punished by Mr. Saavedra, and I am afraid of physical pain. The fear of public ridicule and degradation is no lesser. The names being called are now those starting with E; mine is on the G, and my report card still does not appear. I feel a knot in my stomach, and my forehead is covered with a fine, cold sweat.

I hear "Fernandez!" and after that "Ferrara!" God Almighty! The F is being called out. I am lost! I rummage the satchel desperately, but by now I am so nervous that I search through the same places over and over, so discomposed that even if I saw the blessed report card I might not recognize it.

It is now the feared instant. My name has arrived.

"I'm sorry. I don't have it."

Mr. Saavedra looks at me, as two flashes of white light shoot out of his round spectacles. "Approach," he says.

I approach the desk. The teacher is grasping a long, flat wooden ruler by one end. "You know what to do," he says matter-of-factly.

I know. I extend my right hand, palm upward. He lifts the ruler high above his head and discharges a strong blow. I cannot help it: as the ruler comes down, I withdraw my hand by a protective reflex. I am faster than my punisher. His ruler fans the air and misses the target, much to the amusement of the class. This, of course, is not a rare occurrence, but it never fails to irritate our *domine.* Mr. Saavedra has a stereotyped comment after such foiled attempts: "The next one will be harder." As I know the man means business, I force myself, by a supreme effort of the will, to maintain my hand in the way of the descending ruler on the second attempt. A swish is heard as the straight instrument cuts the air, terminating in a strong clap that reverberates in the classroom when the flat of the wood strikes my palm. At the same time, an intense pain, as of a burn, grips my right hand.

I go back to my seat, very fast, straining mightily to contain my tears. I cover my face with the back of my uninjured hand, in order to hide my contorted, intensely flushed face—utterly discomposed by the grimace of imminent weeping—from the malevolent glances of my amused classmates. But I cannot resist it any longer: the stream of tears pours out, pushed by the mounting tide of sobs that fill my throat and convulse my chest. As my seat is in the back row, I derive some solace by telling myself that I did not cry in front of the whole class.

After the entire roster is called and the ritual of the morning punishments is completed, I have regained my composure. The teacher then orders us to take out our notebooks and geography textooks. To my great surprise, I discover my signed report card inside the cover of my textbook. A wave of righteous indignation polarizes my whole being: I have been punished unjustly. I have suffered for a fault that I did not commit. My first thought is to somehow reveal to my tormentor the unfairness of his act; to make him feel remorse for having maltreated an innocent student; to show him the rashness of his system, the injustice of his ritual of punishments, by which pain and shame are inflicted upon those who, on closer examination, turn out to be without fault. Impelled by this sense of outrage, I stand up with my report card in my hand and tell him: "I had it here, sir. My report card is here. I had it with me all along." Alas, I see no expression of remorse or confusion in his face. He does not appear sorry, not in the least, for having laid a cruel hand on a blameless victim. His recalcitrancy is unchanged, even as outraged justice addresses him. With a gleam in his spectacles and a scornful smile on his lips, he says, addressing the class: "You see? He shouldn't have been hit. But he just loves disorder!"

And I sit down, amidst the unwholesome merriment of some of my classmates. Insult added to injury: to be punished without reason, then exposed as a nincompoop. Learning, I say to myself, can be a most ungrateful experience.

Coming home at the end of each day was a great relief. A long, circuitous route in a crowded, overheated school bus, full of unruly children under deficient supervision, was a daily vexation. But the bus took me away from a detested place of still greater annoyance. I would come home to relax, and to play with my three Jewish friends, for many years my only friends, Leonard, Moses, and Jacob. The latter, five years my senior, maintained the offhand manner proper to those who feel themselves evolved from an immature, childish condition into a higher and worthier station. Indeed, a five-year age difference, though indifferent in adult life, weighs heavily upon childhood. He participated in our games sparingly and, when engaged in them, was apt to play first fiddle. The other two brothers were much closer to me in years, a circumstance that greatly enhanced the daily hobnobbing and unreserved familiarity that followed.

Togetherness with my little friends was not as assiduous as it had been before we were registered in different schools, but a kind of sodality persisted undisturbed. Bonds of amity so early established are not easily dissipated. Furthermore, the friendship between our mothers contributed to foster the occasions for fratting. There were outings, to which more and more I went unaccompanied by my mother, who had begun to work; she became the main breadwinner in the household after my father's rash business activities led to the loss of all our property, including the building we lived in.

Years went by amidst these routines. Life proceeded undisturbed by any truly unusual occurrence. Then, one day, it happened. I mean the eclosion of Moses' intelligence: an extraordinary phenomenon that we were privileged to watch at close range. It coincided with puberty: we must have been about thirteen years old when it first became evident. I recall his keen interest in electricity and electromagnetism. I remember his talking to me about the direction of forces in an electromagnetic field, then proceeding to demonstrate it by means of metallic filings placed on a card, a magnet underneath—an elementary demonstration, which, however, could not have been made with such lucidity and contagious enthusiasm by the teachers of my expensive school. I also recall his pestering his parents until they got him a correspondence technical course on television receivers and electrical apparatuses. But these initial gropings were soon left behind. From surface to depth, from technical aspects to theoretical foundations, from basic concepts to ever more abstract areas of electronics, his progress was as relentless as it was astonishing.

He was not what is called a "child prodigy." There were no outward manifestations of a truly precocious intellectual development. Theretofore, he had behaved like any of us. He had played with us, got into rows with us, shown the same childish propensities as the rest of us, his contemporaries. To see a boy kindled with enthusiasm for a scientific discipline at thirteen is gratifying to his teachers and heartwarming for his parents, but it cannot be said to exemplify a breakage of the normal order of things, a kind of anomaly, as does precocity. Rather, it was as if the cogwheels and springs of his intelligence had been impeded from proper operation by some sort of obstacle and this impediment had been suddenly removed, and the whole wondrous horological mechanism, now unencumbered, set itself in motion, revealing all its stupendous, fascinating complexity. Or as if his intelligence had been a key that he had formerly tried against a number of locked doors and found the trials always boring, regardless of how successful; and all of a sudden he came across a lock so exquisitely conformed to his key that the mere opening of it was a pleasure in which he reveled ecstatically.

These are some of the metaphors I feel compelled to use, for lack of a good definition of intelligence. The experts disagree among themselves in this regard. Some say that it is a complex faculty, with parts or components; not a single ability, but an aggregate of mental properties, such as perception, memory, abstract reasoning, and the capacity to apply these in solving problems. Others assert that there are, in effect, "multiple intelligences," such as spatial, musical, bodily-kinesthetic, and logical-mathematical. Be that as it may, most of us think of the latter, the ability to think abstractly, as the epitome of intelligence, the mental feature upon which our species has traditionally based its pride. This is precisely the mental faculty that surged abruptly with exceptional vigor in my friend Moses.

It is not idle to dwell at this juncture on his Jewishness. For a very close rapport has existed for some time between intelligence and the Jewish people. The sort of approximation that led Charles Lamb to write in a distinctly prejudiced essay: "I never heard of an idiot being born among them." It is a hackneyed proposition that Jews, who form only a small fraction of the total world population, have produced many of its most excellent minds. Not merely competent professionals or proficient experts, mind you, but the truly superior eminences, the paragons that open new fields of scientific exploration and become cynosures for others to follow. To recollect this leads one to conclude that Jews have received a disproportionate share of the world's apportionment of intelligence.

It is likely that the extraordinary flowering of the Jewish intelligentsia has causes and determinants that can be understood and accounted for logically. For one thing, it is not unprecedented. An obvious parallel is found in ancient Greece. In a little area of the Aegean Sea, no larger than certain counties in the present-day United States, and out of a population that could not have been greater than a tiny fraction of that contained in any fair-sized American metropolis today, arose, in a relatively short time, some of the greatest artists and intellectuals of all times. What they did in sculpture and architecture is there for all posterity to see. The Greeks invented mathematics, produced the greatest epic poets, masterly tragedians and comedy writers, and, above all, the foremost philosophers. Other peoples bred saints, mystics, or visionaries. Greece alone opened the way for speculative thought untrammeled by asphyxiating orthodoxy. The Greeks formulated all the fundamental questions, once and for all. What is now debated was already argued at the time of the pre-Socratics. Western philosophy has since been, as Alfred North Whitehead remarked, "a series of footnotes to Plato."

So it is that scholars used to speak mystically of the "Greek miracle." But it is no more necessary to appeal to the portentous to explain the surge of Greek civilization in ancient times than it is to invoke genetic superiority to account for Jewish genius today. And this does not preclude certain gifts and felicitous dispositions in the people or race that produces the exceptional intellectual blossoming. Further, there are cultural features and social conventions that foster this flowering. In the Jewish people, these include a long tradition of respect for learning. The scholarly man, the man who knows, is held into high esteem by the community and enjoys general approbation.

Accordingly, my friends' parents were delighted. God seemed to have blessed them bounteously, giving them an amiable, kind son who now, to their infinite joy and the unmitigated admiration of society, gave proof of uncommon genius. For his gifts bordered on genius, indeed. He completed the requirements toward an advanced degree in electronic engineering in less than half the time that was customary. He encountered some opposition from a professor who, alleging that the young man had not attended all the laboratory exercises, objected to the school's issuing a diploma. Moses, by then very conscious of his powers, olympically replied that he knew more than the professor and consequently deemed it senseless to spend on those exercises the time that could be used more profitably elsewhere. My friend perhaps turned a bit vain, but who could blame him? He could back his boasting. He felt the inner strength that supported him. Therefore, he extended his pinions and confidently soared to amazing heights.

I saw him less and less. I still came into his apartment with great freedom but now looked for his younger brother, Leonard, whose sanguine, even temper, joined to a somewhat cynical bent, made him a congenial fellow. As to Moses, he was either absent or utterly absorbed in his studies. Commissions of distinguished scholars came and went, looking for him—an unusual spectacle in our neighborhood. He was not quite twenty when he received strikingly lavish offers from transnational corporations that wished to avail themselves of his talents.

On one occasion, I stopped by his desk, on which lay an open book. It was a formidable text, written entirely in mathematical symbols. Now and then, amidst the equations, I could spot the occasional paragraph written in ordinary language. Curious to see what the topic could be, I was stopped cold by a statement that said: "Stationary states are conceived as proper solutions of a fundamental wave equation, obtained by regarding the Hamiltonian of a system of electronic particles as a differential operator acting upon a function of the coordinates which define the configuration of the system." My curiosity ceased immediately. Only a few years before, my mother could say: "Why don't you ask Moses to come down and look at our television, which seems to be malfunctioning?" Now such a request would have been like asking Louis Pasteur or Jonas Salk to make a house call to see a child with a mild cold.

Moses' father happened to notice my curiosity at the open book. Usually a quiet, demure man, this time he could not repress a boastful fatherly pride. "This," he said in his accented diction, waving the book in his hand and flipping its pages in the air, "is what Moses studies these days. Quantum mechanics. The general theory of relativity. The physics of elementary particles. The stuff it takes brains to go through . . ." And as he said this, he tapped his forehead vigorously with one hand, as if to stress his reference to all that exists inside the cranium. Then he added: "In order to master certain subjects, all that a man needs is buttocks"—and as he said this, he waved the book in his right hand, while slapping his own buttocks with the left. "I mean the patience to sit down on one's fat behind, reading for hours and hours. But what my Moses is doing is an altogether different thing. . . ."

The quip was unkind. It was, I believe, an allusion to my expressed preference for medical studies. Señor Natán had decided that learning medicine is strictly a matter of diligent plodding and that to gain competence in such a discipline could require assiduous application but, in contrast to the field his son cultivated, not a great deal of intellectual acquirements.

Good Nathan! He was not to blame. He was brimful of fatherly pride. And this pride was wholly justified. His young son was destined to be a flaming star in the firmament of science. All the indications were there. A famous American university had already invited the young man for an extended visit. The entire Jewish community watched his meteoric ascent. And the two parents basked in the glory of the unexpected boon. They had not dreamed of this in the cold, dreary winters of the *shtetl*. Yet unfathomable are the ways of the

Lord. And here, in their exile, they had been endowed with this marvelous dispensation, this wonderful son, this fountain-head of incomparable joy.

Then, in the most cruel manner imaginable, their hopes were dashed. I was at home when Leonard appeared, intensely pale, and said to me: "Moses is dead." Dead. Such was the horrid, incredible word, which we made him repeat twice before we could understand. Next came the relation of the tragedy. He had gone in the company of Señora Clarita to Cuernavaca, about one hour's drive from Mexico City. Dutiful son that he was, he had thought of treating his mother to a restful day at a resort establishment in that pleasant town. He chose to take a swim, while his mother reclined on a low chair by the swimming pool. There was no one else around. In the warm sun, she slumbered. The next thing she saw, upon awakening, was the exanimate body of her son lying at the bottom of the pool. She screamed desperately. Attendants came but could not revive him: he was gone. How long did she sleep? Five to ten minutes, no more. But in the meantime, her son had died.

My mother and I arrived in Cuernavaca at dusk. The lifeless body of my young friend had been laid, at the city morgue, upon a marble-top table and covered by a white sheet. There he rested, still clad in swimming trunks and besprinkled with drops of water, like a fine dew. His eyes lusterless, congealed, and already sinking into corruption, he yet appeared serene and fair. He looked, in his splendid youth, as if asleep. Sleep and death, "the twin brothers," as the ancients called them, never seemed so similar. Homer wrote: "Slumber the deepest and sweetest, and nearest to death in its semblance" (*Odyssey* 13.92). But if the ancients repeated this line to persuade themselves that nothing evil attends the state of those who are dead, we could not help but feel the enormous injustice of his death.

So full of promise, and so prematurely blighted! Snatched hence forever, a mind pure and radiant; malevolently seized by death, leaving his loved ones forlorn, in the pangs of unbearable pain; while the rest of the world could say, with the poet: "We have lost in him arts that are not yet found."

This I cannot forget. We were not blood relatives. And for the last few years of his brief life he had distanced himself from me, absorbed in his world of mathematics and abstract reasoning. But the image of his dead body upon a marble slab, and his hands of ice still bearing a trace of moss, and his young eyes, orbs now gray and dull, though beautiful even as they lapsed into corruption . . . these things I can still see as clearly as on the day I saw them in the twilight, against the mournful cry of a flock of cranes that passed in the sky. These images, joined to the remembrance of our shared childhood experiences, still haunt me in dreams and will follow me as long as I live. And it is well that it be so. For true human affection must cling to remembrance, happy or sad, like the vine to the moldering wall. Nothing more alien to the human heart than to lower the beloved together with his memory into the same grave. Beasts alone love thus: their love is dense, ardent, wild, and of a gripping, rabid quality; but it is also the kind of love that extinguishes itself suddenly, and completely, with the loss of the beloved. Beastly love is long in tears, loud in wailing, grievous in sorrow, but short in remembrance.

This tragic death brutally revealed to me, for the first time, the flimsiness of our lives. In the suffering of my friend's parents I first fathomed the pain of our attachments. I saw his father, haggard, pale, and turned into a different man after this terrible blow. I saw his mother—God! his mother!—sustained by other mourners lest she fall to the ground, crushed by a burden of pain greater than she could bear, and moaning most dolefully. A mere boy I was, yet I most distinctly felt the urge to escape. Starting that day, a recurrent question obtruded in my mind: How can we protect ourselves from such frightful pain? But there is no protection. Whoever loves is vulnerable; and he who loves much is vulnerable in proportion as his love is deep.

Saint Augustine, after painting in the most heart-rending terms his profound despondency upon the death of a friend (*Confessions* 4.10), concludes that it is best to abstain from loving too much what is perishable. And since all things human are transient, it follows that only the love of God is well-placed. That conclusion is eminently prudent; its logic, incontestable. Do not put all your eggs, so to speak, in a defective basket. Love only that which is eternal, imperishable, divine. The prescription sounds all the more authoritative for having been voiced by so great a thinker, mystic, and saint. But is it really worthy advice? Can we, should we, thus manage our affections? What kind of love can we reserve for the things of the world?

The heart would be mummified, or turned to stone, if with each love it adverted to the warning: "Beware, for this love may lead you to suffering." A poor form of love it were, indeed, that needed a contract of "liability insurance" before engaging fully. Which is why C. S. Lewis tells us, in *The Four Loves,* that just as one would never choose a wife (nay, he adds, not even a dog) on such ungenerous premises, just so it cannot be proper grounds of divine love that God offers the greatest security for our emotional investments. No. Advice more to the measure of the human heart is that which says: Love, and love as a man or a woman. In joy and in sorrow. And when fulminated by the first news of the death of the beloved, let the tears stream forth, pressed out by the very force of the blow. Let grief shake your whole body and, compressing the chest, drive out moans and sobs and tears in spite of yourself.

Order, however, must soon be restored. After the first wave of emotion is past, reason's advice must be heeded: do not be extravagant in your mourning. Try to master your emotion soon after the first paroxysm. But later, after a long time has passed, speak of the departed. Search the vanishing images, keep them alive in your remembrance. Go look for them at the bottom of your memory. And if tears come to your eyes once more while evoking the sweet conversations and shared experiences, do not retain them: they will be few. Above all, do not let the memory of the dead fade out and vanish. This is the way of human love, which, contrary to that of savage beasts, ought to be short in tears and long in remembrance.

IV

A
Pharmaceutical
Interlude

$\mathcal{F}$inancial disaster struck when I was about ten years old. The ill-advised affairs and thoughtless business transactions in which my father engaged went finally bust. Of the general debacle I recollect a front-page headline in a major newspaper, with the word "FRAUD" conspicuously capitalized in bold black letters; in somewhat smaller print, the name of my father appeared underneath, along with the names of other participants in a scheme that had defrauded incautious investors. In effect, the ill-fated mining business had caused the ruin of more than a few unsuspecting victims. Greed, I suppose, was no small factor in the recruitment process. For the mines of Mexico were once the source of fabulous riches: silver extracted therefrom largely financed the European Counter-Reformation, the emprises of generations of Genoese bankers, and the military might of the Spanish empire. So what if centuries of continued exploitation had largely exhausted the ore? Such a trivial consideration was not going to quiet the imagination of the susceptible. Mention silver mines, past glories, and sudden riches, and invariably you come across men ready to swallow hook, line, and sinker. My father was among them.

The problem was, he had lent his name and his "legal representation," or his "juridical personality," as they said in forensic jargon, to a fraudulent venture. He lacked the faintest understanding of the mining business, but this did not deter him from founding a "Metallurgic & Casting Company, Inc." Nor was there a mining engineer among his associates. Instead, there were sharpers, fabricators, and cozeners of every description. And now that the finely trumped-up edifice they had erected came crashing down, all the fair-weather friends, from the high strategists to the last backroom boy, absconded as if by magic. The biggest fish maneuvered artfully, in such a way as to make their disappearance coincide with that of the company's monetary reserves. The latter, however, did not amount to much: why, with the steady drain they had been subjected to under my father's inept management and complete ignorance of mining technology, they had in fact dwindled considerably. As for other, less resourceful plotters or more slowly-reacting schemers, there was nothing for them to do when the balloon burst but to suffer public obloquy and to face prosecution or pay damages and indemnities.

To escape this sad lot my father fled, in great haste and under cover of darkness, to his family home in an out-of-the-way provincial village. Once there, he fortified himself behind the bulwark of alcoholism, with green bottles for all muniment. His body protested, announcing by severe symptoms that alcoholic fumes are but feeble rampart against the aggressions of the world. His reply was to seek a deeper and more secure entrenchment: that of the grave, six feet underground. Safeguard without peer, this defense screened him effectively from all present and future threats.

It was left to us, his survivors, to keep the aggressors at bay. For they kept coming at us, sometimes using terror tactics and intimidation. Their bombardments, salvoes, and cannonades sounded: "hereby summoned," "appear at court," and "show cause." The storm troopers were lawyers, notaries, or police officers. On one occasion, they made a raid and took prisoners. A lawyer, an assessor, and a secretary carrying a typewriter knocked at our door, showed us a court order that empowered them to seize property, and proceeded to search the apartment for items of confiscation. They found a collection of handsomely bound books that seemed valuable. These included the works of Tasso, Dante, and Cervantes, in beautiful folio volumes illustrated by Gustave Doré. They pulled them off the shelves, placed them on the floor in a pile, and tied them with a strong string to facilitate transport. I was very young but had grown fond of those beautiful books, more for the illustrations and the fancy leather bindings than for the texts. It saddened me to see so many great artists pulled out of their resting place, roped like vulgar jailbirds, and tied together, as in a chain gang.

My mother walked about, wringing her hands anxiously, during the proceedings. She constantly reassured me, saying: "Don't worry. Don't worry. We will buy back those books. I will make it up to you. Don't worry." The fact is, I was not in the least worried. In contrast to the adult way of seeing things, I saw nothing undignifying in what was happening. Nor was I perturbed by the loss of property. My only grievance was to see what I thought delicate works of art roughly manhandled by uncouth hirelings. But my mother felt some responsibility for the disaster. She had signed papers, much too casually and indiscriminately, at her late husband's request. Now the time for restitution was here, and with it her distress.

In the end, we lost the war—that is, we lost all we had. From landlords we became tenants. And from the posh English School for Boys I was transferred to a public school, where no tuition was required. I went, in a manner of speaking, from one pole to another in the social scale. It was symbolic of the revolution taking place in my homestead that my new school should bear the name Escuela Primaria Benito Juárez, since Benito Juárez (1806–1872) was the Mexican hero who dedicated his life to making his country a democratic republic and to fighting off the ever-renascent threat of foreign domination. In this new learning establishment there was no evidence of fake anglicization; I was in no danger of catching any form of quislingism. My classroom's walls were decorated with figures of Aztec knights battling sixteenth-century Spanish soldiers, leaving no doubt that the philosophy behind the educational effort of the school was strongly nationalistic. And the students were not "daddy's boys," the children of the well-to-do. The majority were poor, and a few were adults of proletarian or rural background, who late in life had come to acquire an elementary education. It was for me a most interesting experience, and by no means the hurtful or traumatic episode that my mother and other commiserating adults imagined.

One asset was salvaged from the general conflagration. It was a small drugstore, whose acquisition had been one of the many flighty business ideas of my father. As it turned out, it was the lifesaver that sustained us in the hour of our need, and thenceforward for many years.

Again, my father lacked the schooling, the training, and even the inclination to become a pharmacist. But such trivial considerations were never known to deter him. He heard that there was money to be had in the drugstore business; and next day, he was busy setting up shop. Not long thereafter, he mounted a publicity campaign to promote his business. A van came and went, with loudspeakers, aimed at the four cardinal points, affixed to its roof, hammering at full blast and with exasperating monotony, for several hours, the joyful news that a new outlet for headache remedies had just opened. The parish priest was summoned for the inauguration and blessed the place. All potential customers were thus made aware that the establishment was launched under the appropriate celestial sponsorship. Moreover, its name was Farmacia Virgen María, the Virgin Mary's drugstore, since it is regular practice in Latin America to name stores by high-sounding appellations: to do otherwise would seem unimaginative and inauspicious. Ours was one amidst myriad stores named Our Lady of this or that, Sacred Heart, Holy Family, and, in more sublunary but still exalted designations, Hope (La Esperanza), Miraculous (La Milagrosa), and so on.

Our drugstore was a tiny shop on a street corner of the barrio, directly underneath our living quarters. It had virtually nothing in common with the efficient, gleaming, modern establishments that are representative of the pharmacy trade in the industrialized world. Ours resembled nothing so much as the apothecary's shop of ancient times, of which it was, of course, a direct descendant. And whereas the ancestry is the same for modern pharmacies, the latter developed new traits, which ours still lacked, and effaced the profile of some that remained sharp in the old-fashioned store of my remembrance.

The place had a front and a rear. The front, open to the street, was no more than fifteen feet wide and about as deep. An L-shaped counter marked the boundary between the space for the customers and that of the working personnel, composed of my mother, an employee, and me. A wooden partition screened this space from the rear area, a small precinct not much larger than a cubicle. This little back room was the pharmacy proper—that is, the place reserved for the preparation of prescriptions written by physicians. Here, shelves placed against the walls supported rows of elegant bottles furnished with stoppers in frosted glass. These flasks contained an assortment of chemicals, whose names were displayed on labels written in pretty calligraphy. One could also see porcelain mortars in various sizes, with pestles to match; a chemical balance inside its glass case, with its pans suspended from the crossbar that bore the dial, and a collection of weights in shiny copper; and there were also spatulas, bowls, droppers, measuring cylinders—in short, all the paraphernalia of the trade was here neatly arrayed.

The ceiling was very high. This made it possible to subdivide the rear area into an upper and a lower compartment, by interposing a boarded floor at midlevel. The upper compartment, to which one acceded via a wooden stair, served only as a storage site. But it had a remarkable feature that I must here relate: in the center of its posterior wall, and apparently built by design, was a large niche containing a plaster statue of the Virgin Mary. Our Lady therefore occupied a place of preeminence, in full view of the clientele—a central and elevated site, as was fitting for the tutelary deity of the establishment.

She was not "the little brunette," *la morenita*, as Our Lady of Guadalupe is familiarly referred to in Mexico. *That one* had already been preempted by the competition. And how! From bakeries to hardware stores, sundry businesses were called La Guadalupana. And her image was reproduced everywhere: on mugs, on windows, on calendars, on storefronts, on dashboards of taxis, trucks, and other conveyances, and even on chewing gum wrappers. Indeed, such were the fervorous characteristics of her votaries' faith that the local brothel in the barrio displayed an image of the Virgin of Guadalupe behind its heavy doors, affixed to a wall of the entrance corridor, with freshly renewed flowers and perpetually lighted votive candles underneath. No doubt these offerings were dutifully maintained by the ladies of the house, whose unique concept of allegiance to the Church did not exclude the performance of a peculiar ceremony after thanking a departing client, which was to make the bills received in payment into a roll and with it trace the sign of the cross over face and chest, while adopting a truly contrite air in front of the venerated image. Let others raise eyebrows and condemn. I say those poor women were in sore need of heavenly protection, since on this earth they had none.

Since we could not avail ourselves of the powerful image of the national deity for our drugstore, we had to make do with a generic one, which was much like the Spanish Virgins painted by Murillo. Her head was covered by a star-studded blue mantle that hung loosely around her body. Her delicate bare feet reposed light as feathers on the convexity of a truncated ball, which on closer inspection could be made out to be the world's northern hemisphere, the southern being hidden by clouds. Her head did not have the circular golden halo that Renaissance artists attributed to all celestial beings. Instead, she sported a neon gas tube that followed her entire bodily contour and emitted a blue glare, accompanied by a constant loud buzzing sound when the switch was turned on, which was done by us every evening without fail, as soon as it became dark. Even though her guise was not that of the mestiza Lady of Guadalupe, her dominant site in our business, and the respect she commanded from everyone, left no doubt that she was, after all, the same divine person. I mean the same one whom Dante, in the *Divina Commedia,* called "daughter of her son" and "humbler and higher than creature" and whom he addressed, telling her: "... *meridiana face / di caritate, e giuso, intra i mortali / se' di speranza fontana vivace*" ("... noonday torch / of charity, and down on earth, amidst mortals, / thou art of hope the living fountain"; *Paradiso* 33.10–12).

Her benevolent protection I now invoke to advance further on the desolate paths of a time long past, and her divine assistance I beseech to resuscitate memories that have lain unperturbed or dead for many years.

Our stock was a curious mixture of folk remedies, herbal medicine, homeopathy, outright quackery, and the resources of official, modern medicine. I may be allowed to know something of this complex trade, since for some years I was not allowed to do much else. I was growing up, and my mother's opinion was that I should help her in the business and share in the activities that ensured our daily sustenance. Consequently, I worked after school as a clerk in the drugstore; some aspects of this interesting occupation I will attempt to describe presently.

A number of ointments were prepared by mixing vegetable grease and various active principles purchased from chemical suppliers. The ointments we dispensed in small wooden boxes about an inch and a half in biggest diameter, with lids of the same material, which we filled with a spatula. The pomade of *pan puerco* (pig bread, a popular corruption of *pamporcino*, Spanish for "cyclamen") was prepared on a base of powdered tubers of cyclamen, a plant of the primrose family that lacks aboveground stems; the round underground tubers, of very acrid taste, are a favorite food of pigs and wild boars. "It is widely used as purgative," says an old edition of the dictionary of the Royal Academy of the Spanish Language, "generally in the form of unguents, since its internal use is dangerous." How topical application of an ointment would exert a laxative effect is something the Royal Academicians do not bother to explain: after all, they were exalted philologists, not physicians, and did not condescend to occupy themselves with such mundane matters. In any case, the neighbors vaunted the ointment's beneficial effects upon numerous digestive disorders. The purists advocated rubbing it on the abdomen, then applying the leaf of a cabbage and keeping it in place with a bandage. I never tried it on myself, because it had a repugnant appearance, for which the epithet "excrementitious" seemed particularly well suited.

Prettier to look at was the ointment named *poligonato*, reputedly effective against sprains, muscular aches, and joint pains. The word inspired me with respect, on account of a certain Grecian air I fancied I detected, reminiscent of "polygonal" and "polygynal." As it turned out, the term was a Grecian impostor: wholly made up and signifying nothing; at least I have been unable to trace it in old medical treatises. But its pretty crimson color was owed to an ingredient whose name made up in romantic evocativeness for what it lacked in Greek genealogy: "dragon's blood" (*sangre de drago*). For a long time, I thought the name was a felicitous flight of the local popular imagination. I then found out that the term is also used in English-speaking countries, to designate a red resin that is extracted from the fruit of plants of the genus *Daemonorops*, which grow principally in Indonesia. Hence the word may come from the Orient. In Mexico there is a plant, technically known as *Croton draco*, that yields the same or a similar product, with which the ointment was prepared. "Dragon's blood" is currently used in the preparation of tinctures for varnishes and lacquers, but, as far as I know, not in medicine. And there has been no modern Saint George to find other uses for it.

Speaking of salves of the ancient pharmacopoeia with suggestive names, I cannot omit mention of "the soldier's ointment" (*ungüento del soldado*). The term, I suspect, alluded to the likelihood of enlisted men's needing it. It was, to call a spade a spade, a remedy against pubic lice. For it is an unfortunate fact of life that practically all mammals may be parasitized by lice (there are exceptions: whales, bats, anteaters, armadillos, and the platypus have not been known to harbor lice), especially if they live in conditions of poor hygiene and overcrowding. Lice that parasitize the pubic area, so-called crab lice, are acquired by human beings, as is well-known, through venereal contact. Consequently, to ask for a dose of soldier's ointment carried a stigma; requests were done always in a hushed voice and preferably addressed to me, the only male employee and of such an age that I might be suspected of ignorance of the remedy's specific indications.

The soldier's ointment was not without its dangers. Its base was calomel (mercurous chloride). Mercuric compounds applied topically may cause severe cutaneous reactions; and sensitization to mercury occasionally provokes bizarre symptoms. When absorbed in sufficient amounts, mercury causes a toxic state characterized by foul breath, soreness of the gums, a metallic taste in the mouth, prostration, fever, and sometimes death from impairment of the kidneys. These serious complications led to the devising of alternative folk remedies, and these eventually were supplanted by highly effective modern insecticides.

The idle, ne'er-do-well types of the barrio amused themselves with jokes about this distressing disease. I recall a sample of their humor concerning the manner of treating crab lice infestation. Their prescription was as follows:

The patient must shave the pubic hair, then lie down in

the sun, spread sand over the lower abdomen, and fill the navel with tequila. These measures are disconcerting for the crab lice, which will react as presently described. First, the heat they experience under the Mexican sun becomes intolerable. This is understandable, since there is no shade to protect them: the forest of hairs that was their former habitat has been shaved off. In the distance, they see a gleaming lake, a veritable oasis: it is the navel, brimful of tequila. Seduced by its appearance, they rush thereto and drink without restraint to assuage their burning thirst. But lo! It was not water, as they surmised, but tequila. Now, everyone knows that immoderate imbibing of this harsh liquor discomposes the mind; those under its influence are often prey to a murderous madness. This happens to the lice: they run amok under the effects of tequila. Then they catch sight of stones and boulders on the ground all around them. For what to us is sand is to them rocks. Impelled by their savage drunkenness, they stone each other to death: not a single one remains standing.

Another therapeutic method, said the jesters, consisted in holding a mirror in front of the patient's pubis. The lice, looking at the reflection, are easily deceived into believing that an alternative habitat is offered to them for colonization. And since the louse is an inveterate adventurer, ten to one that wanderlust will induce a mass migration. The patient is automatically cured when every parasite, to the last louse, leaves the old lair for the sake of the new and untried.

A sensitive reader may feel like questioning the propriety of these anecdotes. I protest that my only purpose is to relate incidents, occurrences, and sayings proper to that old neighborhood as I knew it. Life in a barrio of those times could be depressing and hurtful, on account of poverty and its attendant train of ignorance, ill health, and daily frustration. It is perhaps a measure of the human dignity of the sufferers that they managed to react with humor, however vulgar, to the daunting adversity they faced.

There was no need to be a sociologist to spot the weaknesses of that community's organization. The young did not seem to entertain any thoughts for the morrow. Boys gathered in the street. There was no community center or gymnasium. Youths stood at street corners, laughing and talking for hours, every evening. A pleasant weather permitted this recreation practically throughout the year. Although staid elders of the community disdainfully referred to these youngsters as "vagrants," their lifestyle hardly justified this term. For vagrancy implies a roaming about, a wandering idly, whereas the boys I have in mind were fundamentally stationary. They were "planted" in their street corner, as neighbors used to say, and nightly attendance at their respective corners was an unvarying routine. As the neighbors of eighteenth-century Königsberg could set their watches by the regularity of Kant's daily stroll, just so, at our drugstore, we could count on the gathering of young fellows—and some not so young—at seven o'clock in the evening.

Only a very powerful force, such as feminine attraction, could alter their cohesive immobility. Indeed, when the girls of the neighborhood came out, as was customary in the early evening, to shop for bread, milk, and other necessaries, the corner assembly suddenly thinned. One boy, or more, would leave the group in pursuit of the belle of his thoughts. The girls' sallies were brief, and every minute had to be exploited to the maximum. Not everyone in the street-corner coteries was equally active in this department. Most restricted their activities to ogling. For in those benighted times, when the commerce between the sexes was hampered equally by prudent and irrational prohibitions, a great deal of the compensatory reaction was visual.

That vision's sexual function was overly developed was easy for me to confirm. When our employee happened to be a young and pretty girl, sales took disconcerting turns. Male customers requested cough syrups out of season—that is, when respiratory infections were not prevalent; or else certain liniments and laxatives, formerly in low demand, suddenly grew very popular. It did not take long to figure out the cause of these trends. Proprietary medicaments were arranged by alphabetical order in the shelves. To reach those placed highest, it was necessary to climb a stair close to the counter. Since the use of skirts was *de rigueur* among girls at the time, in the process of the female clerk's reaching out for the desired merchandise, the male customer was gratified with the unobstructed view of a pair of feminine legs. The request was then altered in mid-course: "No, ma'am. Not that one, I mean the next one, to the left..." And so on, in order to prolong the spectacle a while longer.

The subterfuge was soon exposed, and it became my duty, when the requested merchandise was on the highest shelves, to climb the stairs and get it. Needless to say, the demand for the formerly popular nostrums dropped precipitously.

Vision-centered obsession was epitomized by an unforgettable personage, whose story is worthy of being recounted. He was a tall, thin young man by the name of Ubaldo, who was one of the habitués of the street corner directly across from the drugstore.

Ubaldo was in his twenties when I first saw him. Always the first to arrive, he could be counted on to appear every day, except on Sundays, with semireligious punctuality. It seemed plain that he had a soft spot for Marisela, the grocer's daughter.

When she came out of her house for the evening purchases, he would interrupt his animated conversations and look at her in a transport. And her glances, in turn, were of such a nature as might have encouraged any other man to bolder action. But not Ubaldo. He seemed content with merely gazing. Not that he lacked encouragements: the girl smiled openly at him when she walked past, in a slow gait. She even changed the hour of her shopping in order to find him alone and so facilitate his approaches. All in vain. Ubaldo would continue looking and making long, eloquent, lyrical speeches with his eyes, but he held his tongue and remained standing at the usual street corner.

In other places, at other times, the issue would have been very different. Strictly visual relationships—for the existence of this species of affair cannot be doubted—are extremely rare. And the reason lies in their fleetingness: the natural tendency is rapidly toward progress or dissolution. But in this case, unexplainable, arcane influences must have converged that froze the relationship in a bizarre, contemplative state. Both participants were of a strange cast of mind. He would not budge. She would not act. Months passed, then years. And he remained "planted," always at his street corner, rain or shine, as if his feet had grown roots into the pavement. And from that post he continued sending visual emanations full of longing in her direction.

She went so far as to turn down all her other suitors, though it is doubtful that, after years of frustration, she still hoped that any outward behavior on her part would prompt her static lothario into wooing her in the active mode. Their visual exchanges were already the butt of ridicule in the barrio. But nothing happened. He continued immobile, every night standing on his corner, as if trapped inside an invisible cage from which he could not escape. For his problem was not timidity, in the conventional sense of lack of self-assurance. He was a talker, and a vivacious young man. But when Marisela appeared before him, a glass cage perceptible only to himself descended upon him, or a supernatural spell held him in thrall. Then he could only glance wistfully through the invisible walls, without being able to break loose.

It is probably contrary to the most fundamental feminine character to put up with such nonsense for as long as she did. Marisela was strange, but she was a woman, and therefore could be assumed to be more level-headed than her suitor. In the end, long after her silent, strictly visual affair had ceased to be the laughingstock of the neighborhood—years had passed, which robbed it of all novelty—the girl grew tired. She avoided him systematically. Her little sister did the shopping in her place. If forced to come out, Marisela would walk away from her speechless admirer. I hardly saw her anymore: our business lost a customer on account of a mute, longing gaze. And the young man kept on gazing, now in the direction of her window, which was usually closed.

Ten years these bizarre proceedings lasted. Ubaldo had become the doyen of the "corner boys." His merry group underwent many substitutions and defections. Then Marisela moved away from the neighborhood, permanently. I suspect the persecuting gaze may have had something to do with her change of address. But of what could he be accused? He was no stalker, since he hardly moved from his observation post. And if the charge is one of "voyeurism," it must be owned that in his case the visual aberration adopted unprecedented features. To the voyeur eyeing is a surrogate form of possession. Ubaldo did not seem to strive for "possession." Looking was for him, paradoxically, a way of keeping his distance, an abstract form of aloofness.

When he realized she had left, Ubaldo broke a tradition that he had maintained uninterrupted for over a decade: he did not appear at the corner. He missed his "sentry watch," as people jokingly said, ostensibly on account of an illness. It was said he had typhoid fever. Unrequited love, not salmonella, seemed to many a likelier etiology for his disease. He reappeared months later, at the usual site. But he was not the same man. Spiritless, he was unwelcome to the largely renovated coterie of corner boys, and his attendance became irregular, then interrupted altogether.

Thirty years later, on a nostalgic visit to the old neighborhood, I asked my mother if she knew of Ubaldo's whereabouts. He never married, she answered, and this was a fortunate circumstance, because he was killed accidentally. He was struck by a car as he crossed the street. Was it because he was watching distractedly in the direction of Marisela's window? Gossipy matrons said so. But there was no evidence that the accident was provoked by any such lovelornness. In fact, no one knows precisely how the accident occurred in which he lost his life, or what was the state of his visual passion at the time. He took the secret of his contemplative passivity to the grave. All I can say is that he was no philosopher; and yet life had been for him a journey in which he tried, as did Descartes before him, to be a spectator rather than an actor. He was no artist, and yet he succeeded in transforming the gaze, which is intentional, directed, and semicarnal—the eye is the vehicle of desire—into pure abstraction.

Eyes are outlets—"windows of the soul" is the hackneyed commonplace—through which the immanent self can extend its ectoplasmic hands, like unperceived tentacles, in the prefiguration or sketching of an action. This is why there are gazes that caress, others that undress, and some, "like daggers," that kill. Ubaldo—I mean his inner self—went out to the girl of his dreams through the portal of his eyes. But he always returned to himself. Was this from disappointment? No one can tell, but certain it is that his gaze was bidirectional: out and back, a look with a round-trip ticket. His gaze was a circular perversion, a self-sufficient deviancy, an abstract, masturbatory gesture. He did not wait to see himself reflected in the Other's eyes. That would have been tantamount to "losing himself" in the Other's eyes. He chose not to lose himself, and not to lose his gaze, but to recover himself and recuperate his gaze, unchanged, just as before. And therefore the intentionality of the eye was by him frustrated; the inherent property of seeing, which is to reach for the Other, was left by him unrealized. It could have been said of him, who was no artist, what was once said of Marcel Duchamp: that he was the great master of the uncompleted work, the unachieved climax.

V

The Chaos of Life, Seen from Behind a Drugstore Counter

—

I n one of his splendid essays, entitled "The Superannuated Man," Charles Lamb described his impressions upon quitting his job as a secretary in a London firm and going into retirement. After more than thirty years of routine and drudgery, he mused, "I had grown to my desk, as it were; and the wood had entered into my soul." In like manner, when I reminisce about my years in the drugstore, I figure that the front counter, and those shelves crowded with potions and nostrums, entered into my soul. With this difference, though: that Lamb slaved for decades, a prisoner penning down letters, inventories, accounts, and so on—"more folios than Aquinas ever wrote, and full as useful!" he says, with little respect for Saint Thomas—whereas I was the pampered son of the boss. Indeed, Lamb suffered that wearisome servitude which Dickensian London inflicted on office clerks, without much prospect of emancipation. I, in contrast, glad to help my mother in the family business, was spared such irredeemable drudgery. I worked a few hours a day only and sometimes was granted leaves to complete my school assignments.

Moreover, a job in a business open to the general public in a populous barrio is not exactly routine. Colorful incidents abound: many I witnessed that were far from edifying, and not a few of a kind I would have preferred to do without. But they certainly contributed to breaking the monotony. And if one cares to pause and take thought, it might even be argued that the business was not without, in a broad sense, educational value.

My working shift overlapped with the reopening of the stores in the neighborhood, after a two- or three-hour lunch break, as is customary in some parts of the world. A rekindling of activity took place during my work shift. To the general languid torpor, and a silence and heaviness that became oppressive in the hot season, there came a gradually increasing stir, a progressively growing noise and animation in the streets. Then, in the crepuscular twilight, the streetlights went on and the neon signs of the shops began throwing a multicolored glare on the sidewalks. As the evening deepened, shoppers perambulated and hangers-on stood by. Girls went shopping, basket at the hip; and boys, habitually out to ogle the circulating beauties, stood at corners to chat with friends, to tell jokes, and to concoct the various species of mischief that are inevitable concomitants of youth so misspent.

The arrival of peddlers added to the vespertine animation. One of them was Doña Pomposa, or "Pomposita," as she was usually referred to. Her name was an ironic contradiction, since it conveyed a sense of arrogance, magnificence, or, as a dictionary defines "pompous," "exhibiting self-importance" and "excessively elevated or ornate," but she was in fact the very picture of humility and dispiritedness.

Pomposita must have been in her middle forties. She had recently become a widow, and she dressed in black all the time. Actually, this sartorial propensity predated her widowhood by many years. Although living in the city, and in a most populous district thereof, she was in fashion and spirit like one of those women who used to be part of the landscape in rural areas of Mediterranean countries, ladies who constantly wore black and led austere, haggard, recalcitrantly parochial lives quartered by narrow interests of church and family. Oddly, this parched, bleak terrain of her psychological *milieu intérieur* contrasted with her benign, sweet, almost sheepish outward appearance. For she was rounded, short, of ruddy complexion and distinctly lymphatic temperament, a person in whom meekness and low energy combined to produce an impression not only of insignificance but of perpetually anguished worry: Her utterances evoked not the sweetness of the lamb but the pitiful bleating of the lamb about to be slaughtered.

With much reticence, in a low voice, like a child anticipating a reprimand, she had requested permission to set up her wares on the sidewalk just off the main entrance of the drugstore. My mother acquiesced with such alacrity and deferential agreement as left me no little surprised. Then, as if by way of explanation, my mother told me something that perplexed me beyond measure.

Pomposita's husband had been a close friend of my father's. He drove a taxi as the sole and clearly insufficient means of supporting his wife and five children. One night, my father did not return to the apartment at his usual hour. Given his known habits, it seemed justified to surmise that he was out drinking. His friend knew the bars and taverns he frequented, and offered to drive around in his taxi, looking for him. While conducting this search, Pomposita's husband went into a disreputable establishment, precisely as a vicious brawl was starting. One of the brawlers had a gun and fired a shot at the moment that the poor woman's husband entered the premises. He was shot through the heart and died instantly.

This narrative made a profound, indelible impression on me. A man had laid down his life for the sake of friendship. He had been killed, I could not avoid concluding, *on account of* my father's ungovernable proclivities and crapulous habits. As it turned out, my father was not present at the fateful place where the victim's blood was shed. Moreover, no one had asked the man to go searching for his stray friend: his offer to do this was altogether spontaneous and self-generated. But none of these circumstances served to extenuate the feeling I had that my father was guilty and that his guilt expanded progressively, like an oil stain on an absorbent cloth, until the rest of us were in it.

The poverty, or rather the harrowing, abject misery, to which the widow and her five children were lowered after the death of the husband contributed to deepen the sense of culpability that I experienced. I was about seven years old when I visited her place, only a few blocks away from where I lived. My heart sank as I saw their living quarters in one of those multifamily dwellings that were called *vecindades*. These were clustered shacklike rooms that reminded the observer of the grimiest, darkest passages found in the city of London at the cruelest stage of England's industrial revolution; or they could be compared to the labyrinthine, gloomy interiors that Eugène Sue (now largely forgotten, at one time the most widely read European writer of popular novels) described last century in *The Mysteries of Paris.* There was no running water. Water had to be brought from a little faucet outside, which stood at a crossroads of miserable inner corridors. The rooms' walls were made of coarse, ill-assembled wooden boards; the roofs, of corrugated aluminum plates. So was the bathroom, if this name could be applied to a primitive toilet shared by I know not how many families, whence emanated a stench perceptible from at least one hundred paces.

Of the room they occupied I recollect two things. First, a large bed that took up most of the available space. The apartment consisted of that single room, and I suppose the bed was their most valuable possession. It had a brass framework, with a large, shiny brass ball surmounting each of the four posts. Pomposita was petite, under five feet high, and the children shorter still. Hence, instead of lying on the bed head-to-foot, they all contrived to rest on it by the simple expedient of lying athwart its major axis. Six sleepers could thus be accommodated, and rather comfortably, as, good-humoredly, the lady of the house avowed.

The second detail that stuck in my memory was the presence of many bright-red dots on the wall facing the bed. They were so numerous, and covered so much surface, that at first I thought a wallpaper with a dot motif had been used for decoration. But on closer inspection, they were seen to be irregular in size and contour, and asymmetrically disposed. To my utter shock and revulsion, I was later told that those were stains caused by squashing fleas or some other blood-sucking vermin against the wall.

How did this woman—unskilled, uneducated, temperamentally unassertive, and reduced to utter submissiveness—manage to survive? I do not know the dreadful details of her struggle. But she survived and, all things considered, did not make a sorry show of it. For a while, she came every evening to set up her wares in front of the drugstore. Her meager equipment consisted of a five-gallon quadrilateral aluminum can, originally an alcohol container; a portable brazier; and a little stool. She placed the can upon the brazier while she fanned the coals, and a fragrant vapor emerged therefrom. *Tamales*, the steamed corn-dough cakes known in Mexico since before the Spanish conquest, is what she sold to passersby. In the three main varieties, *de chile, de dulce, y de manteca* (pepper-hot, sweet flavored, and filled with roast pork), as is traditional. But contrary to custom, there was no hawking of her wares. She sat silent, wrapped in her black *rebozo*, fanning her brazier, and looking like one of those stoic, impassive women that Mexican painters have depicted crouching immobile at wakes and burial ceremonies, or like stone statues amidst a surreal, arid, cactus-punctuated rural environment.

At the end of her workday, when she had picked up her belongings, or when she first arrived, before setting up her merchandise, she would drop by inside the drugstore for a brief chitchat with my mother. Of a plangent voice, sorrowful in intonation, Pomposita made such remarks as led my mother to say that, much as she genuinely pitied the woman's sad condition, she could not brook her company too long, because of the depressing effect of her conversation. I gather she could have made an excellent professional mourner, had it been her luck to live in a place where this manner of employment was in demand. Granted, she had much to lament. But beyond all justifiable measure, she seemed the very embodiment of rue; all in all, her half-masted carriage, her lachrymatory eyes, her contritely told tales of woe, bespoke something like the constitutional weeper.

It is doubtful that her measly earnings made selling *tamales* would have sufficed to support her large family. But soon the children grew to an age at which they could earn a few pesos.

And here it should be said, to her undiminished praise, that all her children finished a primary and a secondary education, and in due course were able to pull themselves out of the dire, crushing misery under which they languished for years. The time came when they pooled their resources and with the combined income bought themselves a modest house in which the family lived together until all the children married.

I did not do nearly as well grappling with the specter of my father's guilt. This one continued to haunt me for many years. I could not get over the fact that a man had been shot dead because he obeyed a generous impulse; and to make matters worse, that my father had been linked somehow to the origin of this tragedy. It was useless to try to say to myself that the tragedy had been "only" an accident, or "just" an accident. I could not minimize the intensity of the tragic happening.

It is received opinion that the more science and technology advance, the less is it necessary to appeal to mystical or preternatural influences to explain what happens around us. Therefore, I must not invoke the intervention of evil genii, demons, or other malevolent agents. I must believe that my father's friend was killed by a bullet, and nothing else. Such is the message of received opinion. But this is sheer hypocrisy. For if contemporary, science-oriented society did not believe in—and fear—the existence of unpredictable, nefarious forces, the insurance companies would not make the multibillion-dollar profits that they make. Actually, epochs of great scientific-technologic progress regularly experience a parallel increase in fascination with the "occult" and the mysterious: scholars* note that with

---

* See, for instance, Mircea Eliade, *Occultism, Witchcraft and Cultural Forces* (University of Chicago Press, 1976), pp. 58 ff., a rich source of bibliography regarding the attitudes of contemporary industrialized societies toward magic and the "occult."

every strengthening of science and rationalism there is a surge in the popularity of astrology, alchemy, magic, theosophy, and the like. Our age is no exception. Thousands of magazines, and most newspapers, publish daily horoscopes. Astrologers proliferate in American cities; in downtown locales they read tarot and practice palmistry and various forms of magic. President Ronald Reagan and his wife, Nancy Reagan, reportedly consulted a well-known "seer" in San Francisco before making major decisions. The age of the computer has witnessed an explosive growth of interest in esotericism, divination, "channeling," necromancy, satanism, and all manner of "occult" practices.

I would become a pathologist, my central professional concern being to find out causes of death. Were I now to approach the study of the one death that has long haunted me, I suppose I would adhere to methodological orthodoxy. I would ponder every objective detail: the distance from which the shot was fired; the angle described by the bullet's trajectory; the various organs that were injured; their relative contribution to the lethal outcome; and the physiopathologic sequence triggered by the combined injuries. This, I was taught, is called "explaining" a man's death. But after this fastidious reconstruction, I would realize that there is yet one thing left unexplained, and it is the death of *this* man. Why did he, and no one else, come through that door when the shot was fired? What gave my father's friend the idea to go looking for him that night? Why then and there?

Some of us will say that it was fate; some, that it was the inscrutable will of God; still others, that it was "just" an accident. But in any case we would be invoking something mysterious and terrible, a powerful preternatural agency over which we have no control. Chance occurrences take us away from pathophysiology and into the domain of the mysterious, the incomprehensible: a domain familiar to the "savage," where the rule of reason has no place. Here, as a German philosopher put it, the only alternatives open to reason are "extreme reactions" (*Grenzreaktionen*): to cry, or to laugh.* For in the last analysis, life is either hurtful or comic. The chaos of the world may strike us as funny or depressing; but this, of course, implies that we have made an assessment and reached a decision. Before concluding that the world is worth a tear or a laugh, before the evaluation, there is the first reaction. I owe it to my years behind the counter to have some appreciation of the style of this reaction among the urban poor.

In the barrio, there was plenty of stress, crowding, and deprivation. I could tell when the habitual chaos had exceeded its bounds. For there was then much wailing of sirens and much running around of consternated neighbors, and the streets were abuzz with gossip. Then, after the wounded had been picked up by the ambulance and the felonious by the police patrol, there began a parade of wan, trembling, discombobulated eyewitnesses. They came to the drugstore asking for a remedy against *susto*. The Spanish word *susto* means a sudden fright or a startle. However, the connotation of this word has been considerably expanded throughout Latin America. Those who had witnessed an accident or a violent confrontation, like those who had narrowly escaped from serious harm, were *asustados*—i.e., victims of *susto*. Likewise, persons who had been emotionally upset; aggressors restrained from committing violent acts, hence frustrated; malefactors who had actually committed a crime but were now remorseful; and the hypersensitive or imaginative,

---

* Odo Marquard, *In Defense of the Accidental* (New York: Oxford University Press, 1991), pp. 109–29.

who had neither done nor seen anything but had become discomfited after merely hearing of a shocking occurrence: all were equally diagnosed as suffering of *susto*. From what I could gather, *susto* designated any violent commotion of the soul if adjudicated sufficiently severe to perturb the body's harmony and equilibrium.

The definition of this disorder is obscure and imprecise. There is no characteristic, stereotyped set of symptoms and signs that might pass for "diagnostic" of the condition. What American pediatricians refer to as "failure to thrive" falls under the heading of *susto* for those who believe in it. Boys who do poorly in school, like adults (for the disease is not restricted to children) who become estranged from their jobs and relatives, are often branded *asustados*. The believer might even consider a diagnosis of retrospective *susto*: an adult manifesting decreased appetite and alienation from his wife, friends, and relatives could have been *asustado* as a child.

Official medicine, of course, grants no credence to the term. It assumes that all the morbid manifestations described under *susto* may fit equally well under disease categories that are already consigned in modern nosology. Thus the symptoms may be attributable to a parasitosis, or to psychologic depression, or to some other organic illness, be it easy or difficult to diagnose. However, enormous masses of people throughout Latin America continue to be regarded as suffering from *susto* by the laity, or by shamans and practitioners of alternative forms of medicine. Physicians who take care of Hispanic populations would do well to become familiar with this condition. It has already been the subject of serious studies,* which tend

---

* Arthur J. Rubel, Carl W. O'Nell, and Roando Collado-Ardon, *Susto* (Berkeley: University of California Press, 1984).

to indicate that it cannot be dismissed cavalierly as a wives' tale. Disease is a very complex phenomenon, not wholly accounted for in biologic terms. The perception of the community and that of the patient participate in fashioning the concept of illness. Of two patients having the same disease according to the diagnostic criteria of official, scientific medicine, the one who is deemed by his neighbors and friends to suffer from *susto* generally does worse.

What sort of medicament to recommend against a nebulous, some say nonexistent, illness? Why, an equally undefined and questionably effective, medicine. An agitated customer would rush into the drugstore and ask for our anti-*susto* preparation. With the most professional air I could adopt—which, given my youth, could not have been much—I would mix an antacid, carbonate of magnesia, with cherry syrup and distilled water (attention, therapists: 10 gr., 20 ml., and 50 ml. respectively; agitate to form a pink suspension) and place the nostrum in the trembling hands of the patient. It was usually swallowed of a single stroke.

Did it work? In many cases, I am certain it did. It had in its favor the faith of the patient, which has always been a major factor for therapeutic success. Second, it gave the patient the time and opportunity to collect his spirits and regain the lost serenity. Moreover, it provided him (or her) with a sympathetic audience, the drugstore personnel, who had learned by reiterated experience to practice discretion and listen attentively, or appear to do so. And in any case, it could not have done harm, since the ingredients were generally innocuous.

If it had been in my power, I would have liked to remain the observer, the contemplative nonparticipant of the chaos of the world. But this, of course, is impossible. I was then still a child, and I looked in wonder at the world around me. Nor did I have to look far in order to encounter the perplexing spectacle of chaos. The tumultuous, disorderly waves of a world in disarray lapped the very frame of the drugstore's counter. This I could say in a literal sense the day a young lady named Sara came to install her business in immediate proximity to the counter.

In the already limited space of the customers' area, my mother allowed the placement of a worktable. She did it out of sympathy for this young woman, whose modesty she extolled and whose poverty she pitied. Here Sara toiled every afternoon, mending stockings. These, mind you, were the long-gone days when a pair of nylon stockings was considered a precious commodity and guarded accordingly: if a "run" occurred, it was carefully repaired. Sara had asked permission to work inside the drugstore, in a corner of the customers' area where she was sure to get the visibility that would lead to job commissions. And every afternoon, after three o'clock, she would be found in her corner, toiling indefatigably, bent over a sort of metallic cup that she held firmly with one hand. The stocking to be repaired was spread tautly over the cup's opening. With her free hand, deftly maneuvering a hooked needle, Sara would sew the hole.

To her misfortune, she could be said to be rather pretty. A great beauty she was not, however. Poverty, and its concomitant weariness and neglect, had stamped their cruel impress on her young face. She was the oldest sibling of a numerous family and had been forced to work steadily since early in life. Her difficult childhood, and a youth scarcely brighter, were marked by the need to engage in menial tasks for the sake of a meager income. Poverty's harsh exigency dictated the wearing of cheap and inferior clothes; the lack of sophistication and leisure prevented the effective use of adornment or cosmetics:

these shortcomings detracted from what otherwise might have been feminine attractiveness of more than average measure. Yet in spite of all this, when she lifted her face from that mending cup and looked through the window to rest her gaze from the fatigue of her eye-straining drudgery, her large black liquid eyes acquired a dreamy expression that seemed to reflect I know not what sweet, inner tenderness; and when she blushed, a reaction to which she seemed especially susceptible, her mien was as if kindled by a liveliness and a fire that bestowed on her person a unique appeal that was all her own.

One baneful evening, shortly before she was to leave for the day, she lifted her head in weariness and heaved a sigh, over-wrought with melancholy. By chance, Mario, a notorious local hoodlum, had just come into the drugstore, in the company of his wife. He was a fierce-looking man of muscular frame, disordered appetites, and a reputation for dark lust, which in his heart had formed a strange alloy with violence and vindictiveness. Indian features obtruded in his mestizo face chiefly through the eyes and cheeks, by which traits he resembled a Mongol warrior of the steppes. No sooner did he see the young Sara than he was utterly taken. Nor did he care to hide his extravagant admiration simply for being accompanied by his wife.

My mother reckoned it a piece of ambiguous good luck that Mario played the Quixote toward our family. In a barrio, there is no such thing as "privacy" in the conventional sense of the word: personal vicissitudes, triumphs and tragedies, are constantly and most glaringly in the public eye. The occurrences of each person are common property; and the individual, thereby, is made to feel that he is part of the community, a limb or an organ of the living social body. The reversals of fortune that my family had experienced were much talked about. Friends, neighbors, and acquaintances manifested their sympathy. Some expressed support in the shape of quixotic protectionism; Mario, apparently, among them. He violently abused, crushed, and oppressed others but always dealt civilly with us. On occasion, he would come to the drugstore, just before closing time, to see if everything was all right. Our neighborhood was far, in both spirit and physical space, from placid suburbia: not uncommonly, a drunken, disorderly, or otherwise undesirable wight would wander in and give us trouble. Mario acted then in the capacity of a "bouncer"—one so officious and effective that soon we were rid of that plague. Thus it was that from my observation post I could appreciate the dappled nature of the human heart: light and shade, the noble and the vile, alternate therein in a checkered, undissociable pattern.

Mario returned that same evening, this time alone, and attempted to strike up a conversation with the young seamstress. He left without having obtained so much as a quick glance from her.

Icy, indeed, was the reception he got. But he was not easily discouraged. In boldness and lack of scruples he was unmatched. His misdeeds, known far and wide, ranged between petty larceny and armed assault with intent to kill. Nor was it a secret that his various periods of absence from the neighborhood had coincided with restful sojourns in lodgings provided by the state, under lawful custody and by undeclinable invitation.

He reappeared the next day, equally insistent. He sat on top of the very table that the belle of his infatuation was using. She shrank away to a corner, blushing and silent, her head bent upon her labor, while he never ceased to address her, tease her, and cajole her. Stung as he was by her unresponsiveness, his insolence was heightened. There is little question that the man would have turned physical, had it not been for the pleadings of my mother, who tactfully but firmly asked him to leave the poor girl alone. The fact that these proceedings were taking place in a busy public area, where customers of every description came and went, no doubt contributed to persuade him to show some restraint. But he was obsessed. He came back, again and again, much to the young lady's chagrin and our own anxiety.

His vanity wounded, he pressed his brutish suit ever more insistently. In his mind she became the symbolic spoil or booty that he must plunder, and her consistent refusals were to him as many affronts. She had to walk two blocks to catch her bus, and he waited for her when she came out, walked by her side addressing her constantly, telling her jokes after his crass manner of humor, in the hope of eliciting some response. He even tried to pass his arm around her waist, but she pushed him away indignantly and, silent, continued to walk, tears of anger and shame slowly swelling in her eyes.

At that moment, galled by her silence, he snatched her purse away, as if joking, and proceeded to open it to examine its contents. The girl tried to recover it, but he was too fast for her. With a swift motion he placed the purse behind his back, and when she strained to reach out for it, he changed it from one hand to the other. In the course of this annoying sleight of hand, he positioned himself in such a way that when she stretched her arm around him to reach for the purse, the sneak stole a kiss. She repulsed him, pleaded pitifully for the return of her property, and finally broke down crying and sobbing. But he was not about to relent now that, after days of utter unresponsiveness, he had succeeded in making her lose her composure. It was a victory, a brutal victory, like kicking a door open after vain and prolonged efforts to maneuver the key.

Consequently, he took a perverse pleasure in taunting her and provokingly placed the purse just out of her reach every time she attempted to grasp it.

It was also in vain that she tried to recruit the help of passersby. Some did not take her seriously, thinking that the scene was some sort of lovers' horseplay. Others believed her but, upon realizing who the aggressor was, quickly decided that any impulse to assist damsels in distress should be quelled in the bud, immediately and thoroughly. Policemen were, as the saying put it, "notable for their absence." A taxi happened to cruise by. She flagged it down, quickly boarded it, and escaped.

The next day, she appeared earlier than was her custom. She conversed privately with my mother, whom she thanked for having allowed her to set up shop inside the drugstore. The emplacement had given her a good business, with so many women coming in and seeing that they could have their stockings repaired for a modest fee, sometimes even while they waited for a prescription. But now she must leave and was not going to return anymore. The reason was obvious, and nothing else needed to be said.

She knew her harasser lived in the same city block, and asked my mother for his precise address, after being assured that he was unlikely to be there at this hour. In a last act of bravery, she rapped at his door, was received by his wife, and candidly told her of the loss of her purse, begging her help to recover it.

Mario's wife was the fitting complement to her brutish spouse: loud, vulgar, unkempt, quick-tempered, and foul-spoken as the proverbial market woman—the latter not surprisingly, for she had been one. She had left the trade when a heart condition was diagnosed: a hole in the heart, they said, which she made into a conversation piece, even though she had difficulty representing it in her mind. When she heard Sara's complaints, she exploded in a wrathful access of insult and vituperation. The least she called her was a whore. Never did the chaste ears of poor Sara convey as foul, offensive, poisonous obscenities as the mouth of that harpy shot at her in concentrated rapid fire. She accused her of throwing herself at Mario, "like all the others." And her baroque profanities and hurtful expletives were shouted so mightily that all the neighbors within earshot came to their windows to see what was happening. Blushing more intensely than usual, Sara retreated, sans purse or hope of retrieval. And I never saw her again.

The details of this distressful scene I gathered from the halting narratives of the discomposed witnesses who, moments later, came asking for the obligatory beverage against *susto*. The harpy herself came by; and there I was, pouring cherry syrup into the measuring cylinder and weighing carbonate of magnesia in the scale, the same dose for her as for all the others. Meanwhile, she confided her anguish to my mother, thereby consummating what was, probably, the real, effective therapy: "Woe is me, *señora*, that son of a bitch is going to be the death of me!" And she went on with the litany of grievances that she hatched against her unworthy spouse. She had stuck to him through thick and thin, even when he was incarcerated, and how did he repay her? "Bringing his whores into the house!" She, too, harbored a heart that, considered as a moral entity, was dappled: a splash of generous light spots over a dark-hued background of vulgarity. As a material entity, we already knew it to be different by having a hole in it, even though none of us was clear as to what this meant.

Mario and his wife moved away from the barrio. I never knew the reasons, but I suspect too many resentments had been raised locally by his misdeeds and he deemed it salutary to lose himself in the enormous metropolis. It must have been at least fifteen years later that news of him was heard in the neighborhood—news such as to cause a shock with fast-spreading waves of consternation among those of us who knew him. Mario was dead. He had been shot. Mortally wounded by gunshot. Not by one of his many enemies; not by some member of the underworld he frequented; not even by the guardians of the constituted order; but by *his wife*! She, who clung precariously to existence with a hole in her heart, dragged him into nonexistence by explosively boring the like structure into his own cardiac muscle. And she got away with a light sentence, they said, her lawyers having proved that it had been self-defense.

Thirty years after this tragic occurrence, I saw her again, upon the nostalgic visit I made to the old neighborhood. Spending only two years in the penitentiary, she had returned to live with her mother, and stayed in the barrio till the end. She lived a long life, having learned the art of coexistence with a hole in the heart. Of the fiery, violent harpy I knew, there were no visible residues. I saw, instead, a wrinkled, trembling crone who, having heard from my mother that I was "the same boy" who once worked in the drugstore, clutched me by the arm, with a trembling grasp, and addressed me as "child" despite my receding gray hair and bulging waistline.

Behind a drugstore counter, in a barrio of old Mexico, I had ceased being a child. It was, I still believe, a fine site whence to canvass the spectacle of human life in the raw, with its train of miseries, cheatings, deceptions, violence, humor, glory, heroism, sacrifice, and a heavy toll of *asustados*. There was much in it to spoil innocence. How my mother would have liked to see me stay a child! But what filters, what screens, can preserve innocence? What vaccines ward off the universal contamination? Stronger even than maternal love, time works its relentless subversion.

I pulled away from innocence, like everyone, unwittingly. Imagine! Without realizing it, without performing a violent act. There was no conscious activity, no straining, no polarized effort. Strange to recount, we go through the most momentous changes—and this, to my eye, is a most melancholy thing—merely by staying alive. Our being undergoes the profoundest revolutions and transmutations while we do nothing. And just as we age and become "another" despite lying idle—possibly faster for being idle—just so our moral structure is bound to change, even if it were possible to remain perpetually withdrawn in absorbed contemplation, like a quietist monk or an Eastern mystic.

VI

Goodbye to All That

———

*S*usto, owing to the large number of sufferers, must be accounted an important concern in public health. There were other concerns, though — one, in particular, highly prevalent and of clear and distinct etiology, but no less grievous for that: it was love. Distraught lovers, like those who repined under the torments of unrequited or misdirected affection, were also among our customers. In the rack of torture, the sufferer clings to the flimsiest chance of alleviation; none seems farfetched. Likewise, under the pangs of love, the disconsolate fancy that a drug, a philter, or some wondrous resource of the modern pharmacopoeia may serve to slacken the intensity of their torment.

Only the most credulous among the uneducated held such expectations. That my father had had no compunction in exploiting their simplemindedness did him no honor. Poor, superstitious folk, predominantly women of Indian origin newly arrived in the big city from their remote villages, came searching for love potions. Erotic charms, apparently, were part of the stock of drugstores in their faraway hamlets. The first request of this kind had elicited my father's laughter; the second, his greed. The third one found him prepared, ready to draw an aliquot of "love powder" from a duly impressive crystal flask. The fantastic preparation (largely talcum powder) was delivered with solemn instructions for its use:

"Now pay attention. The manner of administration is crucial to its effectiveness. First, you smear some of the powder on your own fingers. Then, when shaking hands with the person you want to influence, or whenever you have occasion to touch him without raising his suspicions, rub the palm and the back of his hand. Rub the powder on softly, and slowly; not roughly, and never in a hurry; and make sure you press on and sustain the pressure for at least five seconds, to ensure the maximum effect. . . ."

My father would demonstrate, adopting a priestly tone: "Like this, you see, slowly, softly, repeatedly . . ." I like to imagine that he became at these occasions a shaman, like one of those magicians of ancient Greece who practiced erotic incantations set upon elaborate ritual acts known as *agogai*. These rituals, or spells to secure erotic domination over others, survive in a collection of ancient papyri written between the second century B.C. and the fifth century A.D., the *Papyri Grecae Magica*. Cultivators of *agogai* knew how to send dreams, how to take away the sleep of another person, and how to make him, or her, think constantly of one individual. I am sure they spoke not very differently from what I heard as a child:

"One application is usually not enough. Two are the minimum necessary. On the first one, as you rub the 'love powder' on, make sure to look him directly in the eyes and say to yourself, 'You shall be mine,' three times. On the second, breathe deeply, draw the air deep into your lungs, while your hand is still contacting his, and keep applying a gentle pressure."

Alas, my mother never thought of my father as one of the "blessed initiates" in the interpretation of magical papyri or the implementation of *agogai*. To her, this behavior of his was an arrant swindle, and she told him so: "You ought to be ashamed of yourself! These poor, ignorant women spend on talcum powder the money that could feed them one whole week." To which denunciation his sly answer was: "Food is not their concern; to the lovelorn, feeding is a low priority. I give them a remedy for what ails them. . . . Yes, a remedy, and an effective one. For if the man has not paid attention before, he is bound to reconsider after all those suggestive hand contacts and squeezes and sighing glances." My father was probably right.

He was not the only one to exploit the gullible. Nor was his style of exploitation the worst. After all, topical application of perfumed talc carries no deleterious effects—excluding, of course, those of the lovesickness it was purported to induce, an effect that, on occasion, I have no doubt it brought forth. Other practices of the barrio's pharmaceutical trade were riskier and plainly unconscionable.

Quinine preparations were sold over the counter, and self-medication was rampant. Quinine, the main alkaloid obtained from the bark of the cinchona tree, has been known for its anti-malarial properties for at least three hundred years. Up to the beginning of the twentieth century, it was the only remedy against malaria, and a widely used analgesic and antipyretic in other febrile disorders. Less well known, and scientifically intriguing, were its actions as abortifacient. When administered to a pregnant woman (for apparently this effect is observed only in the pregnant), quinine causes contraction of the uterine musculature, which can lead to abortion. Official medicine never made use of this property—for instance, in cases in which induction of labor is indicated—because of the drug's unpredictability and erraticism. Very high doses may be required, too close to toxicity to be of clinical use. Yet in our neighborhood there never was a dearth of women desperate enough to try quinine, or of suppliers corrupt enough to procure it. Women who had cause to fear pregnancy resorted to this drug under a variety of forms, such as infusions, powders, syrups, tablets, douches, or intravenous injections.

I recollect, as if it had happened yesterday, the day our chief competitor, Don Nicanor Puente, proprietor of La Guadalupana, a drugstore only two blocks from ours, appeared in person to buy a box of ampoules of injectable quinine solution. This personage merits some preliminary remarks. In the first place, it should be understood that to refer to him as "our competitor" is only a figure of speech. For although he was, in truth, the proprietor of another establishment in the same commercial line as ours, and hence potentially in a tussle with us for clients, the man's idiosyncrasies and irregular business practices disbarred him effectively from becoming a serious contender.

His shop was in perfect harmony with his attitude. Picture a dark enclosure, on account of the shades being always pulled down; a deserted, minuscule customers' area; and, against the walls, rarefied, ill-provided shelves in which empty intervals exist between dusty bottles of elixirs and tonics bearing faded labels. Flimsy cobwebs bridge these voids and somehow seem fitting decor in this desolation. If you watch attentively, you may surprise, down at floor level, a small, dark-furred presence scurrying swifly against the wall, like a shadowy exhalation: it is one member of the family of mice that currently tenants a hole near the storefront's right-hand corner. Their pelletized feces litter the shelves, so that Don Nicanor, in the rare occasions when he must reach for merchandise, feels compelled to cast aside the small particulate droppings by a brushing movement with the side of his hand and, after this maneuver, grasps the item to be sold, brings it close to his face, and blows vigorously upon it to dust it off.

My description is not quite complete. If truth be told, Don Nicanor would have tried to sell the murine feces too, trying to pass them off as pills with extraordinary therapeutic value. In this he would have resembled the fabled alchemist and precursor chemist of the Renaissance, Paracelsus, who is said to have disputed with a canon over the payment for three tiny pills as small as the droppings of mice—*tres murini stercoras pilulas*—alleging their effectiveness against gout. I have no doubt that Paracelsus would have felt at home in Don Nicanor's drugstore; why, with tinctures and "essences" and extracts of plants and botanical products, and so few customers to distract him, the great Paracelsus would have had time to engage to his heart's content in his "calcinations, coagulations, sublimations, separations, and distillations."

The place is habitually deserted. Don Nicanor is often in the bar across the street. Thence he sends periodic glances toward his store, in case a customer might, by sheer accident, unexpectedly appear. Or else he is in the back room of the drugstore, conversing animatedly with friends from his hometown who come to see him very often. In these reunions he is likely to be playing dominoes. No one would presume to become a regular customer, properly so called, of this establishment. But on occasion, a taxi driver needing some change, or a child sent on an errand, or someone too lazy to walk to the next store, could, unwittingly, wander in. In that case, the accidental customer would be likely to encounter an empty storefront, would hear Don Nicanor's exclamations, and his merry friends' loud rejoinders, and the sharp clatter of the dominoes as they hit the tabletop. If the would-be customer was of a type not easily discouraged, he might venture a "Hello?" and "Is anyone here?" and so on, until Don Nicanor appeared, visibly irritated for being pulled away from his favorite pastime. He would hear the customer's request, and depending on a number of circumstances, he might decide to say that he is out of the product asked for, so as to return immediately to the game, or comply with the request in the most perfunctory manner while making it known by a hurried, anxious demeanor that he, licensed pharmacist that he is, is presently much more worried over an ongoing game of dominoes, and the risk of being cheated when not looking, than over the ways to apply his professional skill to the lofty end of alleviating human suffering.

Ordinarily, the sanguine do not survive in commerce; and their downfall is only hastened by shoddy salesmanship. But Don Nicanor managed to eke out a meager living, and to him this was quite enough. He stayed in business against the time-honored tradition that counsels entrepreneurs to build a large clientele. As for him, his preference was to catch a few naive and ignorant customers, without moving a finger to attract them. No simile seems fitter than that of the spider lying in wait in its web to trap the careless insects that fly its way. So did our man wait passively in his darkened store, to exact from each artless victim a disproportionate, outrageous profit, through all the shameless and deceitful stratagems he could think of.

This time, he had come, as I said, to buy from us a box of

injectable quinine ampoules. He addressed my mother in his usual ceremonious way and requested that the ampoules be soaked in lukewarm water. I proceeded to carry out this odd request, and in the meantime I could overhear his conversation with my mother:

"Ma'am, I don't pretend to tell you what to do in your business. But you deserve better than to struggle for a pittance, as you do now and have done since your husband passed away. You will forgive me for saying this, only I can't help but seeing that you could make a bundle, if only you made up your mind to it, considering that you have a large clientele. Take these ampoules, for instance. I am going to resell them for ten times the price I buy them from you. And you could sell them for twenty times the marked price, without any trouble. . . ."

"Don Nicanor, the government has set down strict regulations, you know?"

"The government! Excuse me, but they could not care one jot about us. They allow the big pharmaceutical firms to take in incredible profits yet woe to us little guys, if we should dare pocket a few cents! . . . As for me, if an inspector comes by, all I have to do is hand him discreetly a wad of bills. They are all on the take, as everyone knows. And I still come out ahead in this game. . . ."

"Still, the regulations were created to protect the public. The people here are very poor. . . ."

"Poor they may be, although I bet they are not as poor as you think. They seem to have enough to squander every payday. And how about you? You are not in clover, let me tell you. You have two children to support and have had a rough time, if you'll pardon me for saying so, ever since Don Pablo, your late husband, was called away by our Maker. . . ."

In short, he had asked that the ampoules be soaked in

water so as to make it easier to remove the labels; and he was going to affix new ones, of impressive German format, in order to resell the merchandise at an exorbitant price to the credulous customer whom he had promised "a most effective new medicine, imported from Germany, due here very soon."

After he was gone, I asked my mother: "Will you take his advice?" She paused only for a few instants and answered: "I couldn't. I feel my face would fall off, for sheer shame, if I ever tried such things. But you shouldn't be eavesdropping on grown-ups' conversations."

It was shame, in her words, that stopped her. Laudable as her example seemed to me, Aristotle might have questioned it. For the Stagirite states, in his *Nichomachean Ethics* (4.9), that shame is not a virtue or excellence but an emotion that arises secondary to the voluntary performance of base actions, either in deed or in thought. And since the wise and decent person does not commit base acts deliberately, nay, does not even think of committing them, it follows that the emotion of shame ought not to exist in such a person. Shame, says the philosopher, is tolerable only in the young, who are often controlled by their emotions, not by right reason. From all of which I gather my mother was still young at the time, or else the Aristotelian system of ethics is inhuman. My mother was not perfect, in the same way that I was not perfect and Aristotle himself was not perfect. No one is perfect, not even the blessed saints, with one foot already in paradise and the seal of holiness shining upon them. In the whole history of humankind, there has never been, there cannot be, and there never will be an individual who properly may be called perfect. Not only does perfection fail to be concretized in any individual, but it is impossible that it should exist in this world. It is inconceivable as an entity of objective reality, although we are compelled to admit that it exists somehow, somewhere. It reminds me of nothing so much as those geometrical figures that Plato's personages are fond of invoking in his *Dialogues*, such as their much-quoted ideal triangle: no example can ever be found in nature, yet we are made to believe that it exists somewhere, since it has fixed properties that geometers can independently—and conclusively—demonstrate.

This imperfect world, however, was changing very fast, and our own society was not excepted. To safeguard the health of a very rapidly growing population, strict laws were imposed. Drugstores had to be under the direct supervision of properly qualified professionals—that is, persons possessing the appropriate training and education, as evinced by a degree in pharmacology, biology, biochemistry, or some other pertinent discipline. How could we, in the barrio, comply with the new stipulations? My mother lacked a higher education: she had survived the revolution under circumstances so harsh and irregular that she was lucky, indeed, to have attended elementary school, however discontinuously. Many other pharmacies were in the same situation, headed by shopkeepers lacking the professional preparation that was now demanded. In the postrevolutionary confusion, people had ventured to make a living in whatever manner seemed possible, and some of the more enterprising had seen fit to enter the ostensibly profitable pharmaceutical guild, at a time when the conditions of admittance were relaxed. The law now decreed that only competent professionals could take up this risk-laden occupation.

To stay in business, we had to hire the services of a qualified pharmacist, who would be "responsible" (this was the official designation) for the technical aspects of the business. For a small commercial concern such as ours, with earnings barely sufficient to maintain the day-to-day operations, the additional expenditure was quite onerous. But it could not be avoided: the regulations had been issued in imperative terms. Then a solution was found: a lady diplomate, a biochemist, agreed, for a relatively modest fee, to lend her name and representation to our firm. Name and representation were meant literally: the bargain did not include her physical presence. She was well aware that, by law, she was supposed to be present every working day for several hours. But we were made to understand that no graduate of the university and diplomate of the professional schools would have actually complied with the requirement for such meager emoluments as we had agreed to pay. To raise the stipend was out of the question, and she knew it. Meantime, she could be summoned by telephone, if needed.

Our "responsible" officer took on an exemplary character. My mother never ceased to impress upon my sister and me that the acquisition of a superior education was the key to freeing oneself of such humiliating and fatiguing burdens as she had been forced to bear. Nor did her injunctions fall on deaf ears. I could not fail to be impressed, at the time, by the power of a professional's diploma. It seemed to me that a diploma of the university, in fine vellum, was a magical tool that bestowed on its possessor a kind of miraculous immateriality and immanence. This was beyond question, since the biochemist could be at home and yet her actual presence did not cease to reside in the diploma, a copy of which was conspicuously displayed in the drugstore. It also conferred the gift of ubiquity, since the lady diplomate sold her services to many other drugstores, and the hours posted at the different locations overlapped. She was thus like Saint Nicholas of Patras, who could be at one and the same time sitting upon the episcopal throne in his hometown and assisting sailors in distress on the open sea; or like any of a number of other saints who manifested the portentous gift of ubiquity, as quaintly consigned in *The Golden Legend* and other works of hagiography.

These irregular practices were widespread, and soon the government caught on. Stricter regulations were issued. A competent professional, a card-carrying pharmacist, must be present at all times. Unannounced on-site inspections were implemented, which sent my mother trembling and blushing every time. Our "responsible" diplomate lady remained a purely immanent, disembodied presence. She never materialized when needed, although she condescended to appear in the flesh once a month, to receive her pay. In a system of widespread corruption, however, the sanctions stipulated by the well-meaning decree could be waived if one greased the willingly extended palms of complaisant inspectors. But each new exaction was a serious blow to the very integrity of our business. We were going under, it seemed; there was a real danger of losing our only *modus vivendi*. Life is never easy, but under the sign of fear it became ever harsher. The stigma of apprehension, of ever-present worry, visibly darkened my mother's formerly serene countenance. Perpetual mistrust and constant uneasiness, exacerbated by episodes of acute anxiety during the visits of corrupt inspectors, relentlessly took their toll.

We thought we had reached the end of our rope, when a more enlightened legislation was enacted. Seeing that a significant number of small businesses were being brought to ruin, the Ministry of Health contrived the means to capacitate those who had learned their trade empirically, without the requisite formal schooling. There would be an examination for eligible candidates. Those who passed the test would be granted a special diploma that entitled them to the designation "auxiliary to the responsible pharmacist." The need for a "responsible" professional was not abrogated: it would still be necessary to pay for the services of a qualified individual. But it was understood that the latter would furnish professional support and that in his or her absence there would be an "auxiliary," with the minimal knowledge necessary to manage the drugstore.

I am always deeply moved when I evoke the days that followed. My mother applied for the examination. Unschooled, buffeted by a life of deprivation, overworked, and confronted by hostile forces, she now readied herself to defend her only means of survival and that of her children. The obstacle in her way was, in effect, an academic hurdle: she, who never trod the halls of an institution of higher learning and never dreamed of scholarly attainment, was now to undergo oral and written tests. But much was at stake, and she was ready to face any obstacle. Life had been her teacher, and by haphazard, desultory experiences and readings she had picked up the rudiments of her trade. Now she was supposed to demonstrate her proficiency to real experts, to university-educated professionals. She was to sit in front of the professoriat; she, an adventitious member of their discipline, was to be quizzed by the learned members of the establishment.

The thought of the approaching date was an added stress in her difficult existence. Even during the discharge of her daily routines, she carried with her the notes she was trying to memorize. Late in the evening, exhausted after a full day's work, she would review the manuals and texts that the examiners had recommended, and would fall asleep on the open books. I was a pubescent boy, already able to help her. Many an afternoon, between customers, she would ask me to quiz her:

"Shall we do synonyms, Mother?"

"All right."

"Phenazone?"

"Antipyrine!"

"Good. Phenacetin?"

"Acetophenetidin!"

"Fine. Aspirin?"

"Acetyl-salicylic acid!"

"Adrenalin?"

"Epinephrine!"

"Mom, you know them all already. Now tell me an agent anti-amebiasis—"

"Emetine!"

"—that starts with a *C*."

"With a *C*? Wait . . . wait . . . don't tell me! With a *C* . . . Is it Carbarsone?"

Thus passed days whose mere remembrance fills me with I know not what curious mixture of tenderness and melancholy. An adolescent boy and his mother, who was beginning to look matronly, stood side by side, their lives gliding on together. The mighty blasts of life had yet to scatter them apart, like leaves in the fall; their two destinies seemed still woven in one.

She passed her examination with flying colors. What paean would render her due tribute? I would fain sing one, if only I could find the words. "Auxiliary to pharmacist" was her highest academic attainment! A risible title, from a narrow perspective. Risible? With the deeper percipience of the heart must it be canvassed; not with the eye of sense. And then, what pains, what crosses, what sorrows, can one descry behind that humble diploma! With it for all protection, she managed to shield the freshness of our childhood from the inclement hour. Evoked through the mist of more than fifty winters, her devotion still emerges resplendent; and as I recall her sacrifice, her former self flashes up again in my memory, and I see her answering the questions in the drugstore, smiling. Faded, spent, and old as she now is, I shall see her truest self as long as I live: at once delicate and stalwart, affectionate and tender, maternal and consoling.

If nothing else, her sovereign example left me with an abiding reverence for books. Books, I came to believe, were instruments of redemption. Thence I approached them with the trusting attitude of the faithful facing the sacraments, the vehicles of salvation. My regard for the printed word has since experienced decrement and all sorts of qualifications. It was then the pristine faith of the catechumens; it is now more akin to the fondness of the old philanderer for his young paramour: aware that she may do him more harm than good, yet unable to do without her and prompt to find excuses: "If we all must go, and the road is tough, this at least sweetens the transit."

In the barrio we had neither libraries nor bookstores. The closest thing to a bookstore was a notions shop that stocked also school supplies, including the elementary school text-books in greatest demand and a few cheap novels. Therefore, when my appetite for literacy began to exceed the local sup-ply, I used to walk downtown, some twenty blocks away. There I gazed to my heart's content through the windows of book-stores at neatly arrayed volumes and could come in to leaf through or read the inexpensive volumes set within the cus-tomer's reach. The expensive books, handsomely bound in morocco, were usually behind locked doors. Like beauties of a sultan's harem vaguely seen through barred windows, they made my youthful heart beat faster and my chest heave a sigh at the realization that I could never hope to possess them.

I still remember an incident that filled me with longing

for the unreachable volumes. My maternal uncle had come back from the north, where he had been an agricultural laborer in the *bracero* program (from the Spanish *brazos*, arms, since field workers earned a strenuous living with the effort of their arms) sponsored by the United States government. We listened, open-mouthed, to his tales of adventure, no doubt embellished by imagination and the need to prop with fantasy his self-image, otherwise weakened by a life of humiliation and underachievement. He had roamed as far as Montana and Michigan, hauling crates of tomatoes, picking strawberries, and, allegedly, organizing his less able, illiterate compatriots, whom he taught the art of survival in a hostile, *gringo*-dominated environment. My mother had once hoped that upon hearing of her widowhood and destitution, her only brother would come back to join forces with her against adversity. No such luck. Her brother had seen the fabled *Norte* and contracted a serious case of wanderlust. Furthermore, he claimed, his fellow countrymen needed him, for they suffered the injuries of racism at the hands of heartless exploiters. But the truth is, he still itched to see the world and, more especially, certain feminine presences in it, for which he had a notorious weakness ... but that is another story. For the time being, he was with us, in one of his sporadic visits, between two *bracero* contracts.

Waiting to be signed up, he took whatever odd jobs he could find. One of these was as watchman of a rich man's property, while the owner was abroad. My uncle's impeccable recommendations and affable personality had earned him the full trust of his employer. On a Sunday's early afternoon, we went to see the house at my uncle's bidding. As others go to the theater, or to a picnic in the countryside, my family and I attended the inspection of a rich man's house on that occasion, by way of Sunday entertainment. We were ushered in hurriedly and with deliberate dissimulation, as my uncle was worried that the neighbors might see us and later report to the owner that unauthorized visitors were being received in his absence. This fear was unfounded, since the extensive grounds of the property, and the tall stone fence that enclosed it, effectively precluded the view of the main entrance.

Palatial surroundings, for those whose whole lives are passed in humble quarters, always have a strong, utterly *sui generis* effect. I was not a stranger to luxury. Like everyone during the forties and fifties, I had seen the dreamlike world of ease and affluence that Hollywood beamed, in film after film, to the whole planet. But somehow those screen images never lost their flavor of unreality: they existed captured in celluloid and came to life on the screen inside a patch of light that was a realm unto itself, a separate dimension, halfway between truth and fantastic vision. Likewise, I had read narratives of Oriental luxury in stories and fairy tales. But these, too, were ectoplasmic presences that rose out of the printed pages through the conjurations of the act of reading. Now, suddenly, I found myself immersed in real-life luxury: in the bedrooms, the crimson silk really glowed under the incident light rays; the laced curtains were truly uplifted by the breeze; and the marble floors of corridors, like the fine wood of stairways, actually resounded under our steps. It was an extraordinary, indescribable experience. I could understand the reason why irate revolutionary mobs, used to the meanest lodgings, and irrupting into the royal chambers they intend to burn and smash, are momentarily stayed by the arresting spectacle of grace and beauty that floods their senses.

Nor is this an idle image. All throughout the third world, these jarring contrasts are commonplace. The poor endure subhuman conditions, whereas the rich, living just a few city blocks away, enjoy comfort and privilege beyond description. I had seen a hollow-cheeked widow and her five children dwelling in a single room of a *vecindad* in heartrending circumstances. Now I could see for myself, for the first time, that a corner in the garden of this house, behind latticed gates and with a tarpaulin for a roof, where tools were kept, was many times preferable to certain mean abodes near my barrio, where the poor went unfed for most of their wretched lives.

These considerations notwithstanding, none of us experienced anything like rancor, resentment, or bitterness. We did not feel disconsolate, or insulted by this excess of wealth; nor did it occur to any of us to contrast it with the harrowing penury we had seen in our neighborhood. We felt rather like visitors in a museum or a historical building; or like birds of passage gazing at the rooftops below, conscious that we did not belong there and could not alight there. After we had ejected a sufficient number of "oh"s and "ah"s before the wonders of the princely habitation, my uncle took us to see the library. There, in a stately, quiet room, by the light of painted glass windows ablaze with varied tints, were shelves replete with all the fancy editions I knew of, and more. I had been elated at the prospect of examining them, these neatly gilded, wonderfully illustrated works. To my utter dismay, I discovered that the volumes were placed behind glass-paneled doors, which were shut and padlocked. My uncle did not have the key, and did not know where it was kept.

I went so far as to ask him whether the owner would mind my coming as a visitor and, with his permission, using his library now and then. My uncle did not think this was prudent and commented that his employer was not easily approachable. I ventured to say that he must be a true scholar, considering the size of his library and the superb quality of his acquisitions. To which my uncle answered:

"The man is a jackass. He buys these fancy books by the meter and for the looks of the covers, but in his life he never opened one. I know that for a fact."

"Really?"

"I am telling you, *muchacho*. He is no more educated than you or I. He made his money in the construction business, where he started off as a contractor. Now that he is loaded, he sends his daughter to study in the United States, but she is as little interested in studying as he was."

"So who uses the library? His wife?"

"His wife passed away years ago. She did not read, either. But at least she cleaned the shelves now and then. You can see that these books are gathering dust. And the man does not allow anyone to come near them. What moved him to spend so much money on books he never reads? Beats me. Unless it was to impress his friends . . ."

Indeed, the bookshelves were dusty, and the expertly tooled, wonderfully adorned leather-bound volumes had the look of never having been opened. All the resentment against the rich then came rushing to my head. I did not mind his having a swimming pool when in our house the water was often interrupted several hours in the afternoon. It did not matter to me that there was a squash court for his private use, and none in the entire neighborhood where we lived. But to have such a library and never use it! That, I thought, was an unpardonable crime, an offense of *lèse-majesté* against the sovereign power of the printed word, for which the man should be quartered in the public plaza.

He was a vain and unlearned book collector, a member of a tribe that has existed since the invention of the written word.

Lucian of Samosata, in the second century of our era, casti-
gated such a despicable species in an immortal essay. The
titular "Ignorant Book Collector," wrote Lucian, is like a non-
musical type who thinks that by purchasing the instrument of
Ismenias (a famous flutist of classical antiquity), he will be able
to play well; like a weakling who, having by chance got hold
of the bow of Hercules, expects to draw and shoot straight; like
the timid churl who never mounted and thinks that because
he just bought an Arab thoroughbred, he ought to be deemed
a master of horsemanship. He, adds Lucian, is also like a blind
man who purchases a mirror, or a deaf-mute a lyre, or a lands-
man an oar, or a seaman a plow, or a eunuch a concubine.
Amidst his books, the ignorant book collector looks rather like
Thersites—the ugliest man who ever came to Troy, according
to Homer (*Iliad* 2.250)—in the act of trying to put on the armor of Achilles: instead of looking strong and stout, he looks
ridiculous; he totters under the weight of the helmet, squints
his eyes under the glint of the shield, and deforms the corse-
let with the hump of his back. Such a one is held in contempt
by all. Parasites who expect his favors will praise his learning,
then look at each other behind his back and have trouble re-
pressing their laughter.

All these experiences I left behind. Yet half a century later,
the memory of them surges anew now and then. When arrogant men make boastful displays and send the timid scurrying
away like children frightened by thunder, I evoke the day when
my family and I, fresh from the barrio, learned that money often buys appearance but never buys substance. And other
times, when the unceasing strife and discord of life has made
me weary; when, spent and exhausted, I have felt ready to ca-
pitulate; when instead of the energy to sustain the struggle I
have felt its imminent surcease—then it is that the image of

my mother, looking as when she approached middle age, has appeared before me, engaging me in a rapid dialogue that infuses me with renewed enthusiasm:

"Acetophenetidin?"

"Phenacetin."

"And aspirin?"

"Acetyl-salicylic acid."

For this cryptic dialogue was tantamount to saying that if it is true, as Seneca claimed, that "the life of man is an assiduous war," then gallantry is never to surrender.

VII

Of Free Choice
and Fate

———

S teady, unswerving, with all the unopposable might of
things inevitable, came the day to choose a career. Plainly,
neither my close friends nor I experienced that innate propensity, that sharply focused convergence of psychic energies upon
a specific and irreplaceable goal, which is denoted by the word
"vocation." In its original use, this word meant partiality for the
religious life. "Vocation," from Latin *vocare*, to call, alludes to *vox*,
voice; and there is little question that a voice from on high is
what was meant. Consequently, to perceive a "calling," or a vocation, meant unmistakingly to hear the voice of God sum-
moning the hearer to His service.

A lofty call of this sort I did not experience; nor have I ever
witnessed its mighty instrumentality in others. In our irreli-
gious times, it may be that only artistic inclinations, at least in
some emotive personalities, approach the unyielding, almost

unbearable prodding of a true vocation. What I and my contemporaries felt was a more or less strong fascination with the externals of an occupation: with the glamour and shine, that is, of a liberal profession that had managed to earn considerable prestige in society. This is not to deny that, like all young people, we were essentially generous and idealistic; we fervently hoped to be able to relieve the suffering of our fellow human beings. But the full significance of opting for the life of a physician escaped us.

A career choice is, obviously, a serious matter; one that merits the most earnest deliberation. But the need to make an early choice, on account of the lengthy preparation required, often impels the young to decide in a hurry and to face the consequences of a hasty decision later. That not more frustration and disappointment issue from impulsive entries into medicine is a tribute to the overall excellence of this occupation.

Take Oscar G., one of my classmates. He had manifested a preference for the study of law. His parents encouraged this inclination, and we all expected to see him turn into a fine lawyer. Family, acquaintances, tradition, and personal aptitude: all seemed to steer him into the legal profession. The enrollment in professional schools was less systematic than it is now. Furthermore, in contrast to the extremely rigorous preliminary screening that is customary in North America, huge numbers of students were admitted. The expectation, unfortunately valid, was that their numbers would be dramatically reduced by the appalling rate of attrition that took place subsequently. The initial enrollment, however, was little more than a bureaucratic step, well within reach of all who had completed a few required courses. Thus, on the day of registration, veritable masses of students converged on the campus, each one to sign up in the school of his or her preference. Oscar, to no one's surprise, joined the large cohort that applied for admission to the school of law.

This will explain our amazement when, shortly after courses started in the medical school, we came across Oscar inside the anatomy laboratory.

"Why, we clearly saw you going to register in law school!" we exclaimed.

"Yes," said he. "But the line was simply too long. I was terribly bored. Then, from where I was, on the second floor, I could see that a new window was about to open to expedite registration in the school of medicine. I rushed to the site before the line re-formed, and so became one of the first to register."

The choice of a lifetime made on the spur of the moment, and out of boredom from standing in line! And the irony of it is that Oscar finished the studies so recklessly embraced and became a very competent physician.

Nor is there any guarantee that a more serious approach will ensure success. The life of a physician has unique stresses and rewards; neither can be fully grasped by those with limited life experience. Emotional maturity, insight into human strengths and foibles, commitment to lifelong study, the intellectual flexibility that permits one to learn from experience, the desire to be of service to others and to alleviate suffering, and the capacity to maintain a critical judgment at every juncture, even in situations of crisis: these are attributes that cannot be taught and must be developed, if the germ of them exists already, by long-standing experience and assiduous cultivation. Desirable qualities in any physician, they are indispensable to whoever aspires to excellence in this demanding profession.

But it is a rare young person who will see any of this. And

neither did we; at least not fully. What we saw was, among other things, the not inconsiderable prestige and authority accorded the profession. For authority was still much in evidence in the physician-patient relationship in those benighted days.

"Be it known," says Henry Fielding in the second book of *Joseph Andrews*, "that the human species are divided into two sorts of people, to wit, high people and low people." And although he goes on to say that "high people" is not to be understood as "literally persons born higher in their dimensions, nor metaphorically those of exalted characters or abilities," yet there is little question that in the first half of the present century, the medical profession had annexed the latter meaning to its public image. The therapeutic virtue was conceived not unlike a hydraulic force: in order to flow, it had to proceed from a higher to a lower level. Higher stance, it was understood, resulted from being in possession of specialized medical knowledge. Consequently, the physician's rightful place in the system was higher than that of other technical, specialized personnel. And athwart them, but on a lower stance, was the patient, the passive recipient of their ministrations.

Of late, every aspect of this relationship has come under keen scrutiny. A liberal profession is scarcely to be found that is subjected to surveillance as rigorous or checks as stringent as those that regulate the practice of medicine. The very word "patient" has been said to be patronizing or somehow degrading. (It most certainly is not: the word issues from the Latin verb *patir*, to suffer; and for a long time it was used in a theological context, to express the sufferings—the *passion*—of Christ.) Whatever damage may be laid at the door of the unsupervised practice of medicine in recent years, it begins to be exceeded, at least in North America, by that due to an overly zealous effort in the opposite direction. In this part of the world, the beleaguered physician sometimes feels constrained to withhold opportune and on occasion crucial intervention, out of fear of legal suits; to say nothing of the damage secondary to rising costs (hence lowered availability) of medical care, traceable to extravagantly cautious or punitive regulations.

Physicians are held accountable, often to an unreasonable degree. And patients are enjoined to "take charge," in the measure that this is possible, of their own therapeutic management. Intelligent patients are well-informed of recent treatment innovations and novel procedures. They can question the appropriateness of recommendations, discuss the risks and benefits of medicaments, and request a second, independent opinion, before accepting any procedure of potentially serious consequences.

Yet in spite of all these welcome attitudes, the "hydrodynamic" concept of medicine, by which curative potency resides on a higher level and must flow downward, has proved remarkably enduring. The reason is clear. We hold our well-being, our bodily health, our physical integrity, precious. What! Would we entrust such a priceless possession, such an admirable mechanism, to a *simple* human being? We would no more abandon our infinitely valuable person to the hands of a weak, fallible individual, as prone to err as you or I or the next fellow, than we would expect to see the water inside two intercommunicating vessels flowing from the lower to the higher. Only superior beings are worthy of taking care of us, and "superior" means placed above the average, residing on a higher plane. And if we should discover that those who care for us are petty, forgetful, inattentive, complacent, ignorant, or otherwise flawed in a typically human fashion, our imagination will repair the flaws, substituting intelligence, equanimity, compassion, and, in short, wisdom wherever a limitation is spotted.

There is also the rightfully earned prestige of medicine: the undeniable, spectacular recent achievements of this discipline. A little bit of its resplendent glory must perforce inhere in each of its practitioners. But this power is newly acquired. For a long time the pedantic physician was the obligatory cliché of comedy writers. From classical antiquity to the Enlightenment, the physician often appeared on the stage as a silly, ridiculous, conceited personage, who tried to hide his powerlessness behind Greek or Latin utterances. In effect, his gibberish was drawn from Galenic lore or the Hippocratic corpus, sources now equally deemed ineffectual and stale.

As to the surgeon, he was still more contemptible. He was assimilated among the practitioners of trades that did not require a university degree, like the barbers, from which he was at first indistinguishable. "*Puta, leguleyo, y barbero, van por un mismo sendero*" (Whore, shyster, and barber tread the same path), says a pithy Spanish proverb of the sixteenth century. In a one-act theater play or *entremés* by Miguel de Cervantes, entitled "The Divorce Judge" (*El Juez de los Divorcios*), various plaintiffs bring their conjugal grievances to court, expecting redress. One of them is a woman whose main complaint is that she was deceived into marriage by a man posing as a physician when in reality he was "only" a surgeon. It is telling of the huge impact surgery has made on public opinion that today it would be inconceivable for a woman to base a complaint of deception on similar grounds and hope to elicit commiseration.

Formerly a caricaturesque, puffed-up figure; often hoodwinked, cuckolded, or otherwise humiliatingly dealt with in comedy, much to the merriment of the public, the physician underwent a radical transformation of image. By the last century, the medical man was already a romantic figure, noble and understanding, in popular novels and stories. True, the "naturalist" novelists, mercilessly realistic, made no concessions to the dominating taste and could, on occasion, depict him as bumbling, inept, and cuckolded, as in *Madame Bovary*. But this was only an exception, for the sake of dramatic effect: Charles Bovary is, after all, a marginalized practitioner in some backwoods, a country doctor out of touch with the dazzling advances of the medical science of his day.

That popular culture drew this improved, flattering picture of the medical professional no doubt influenced youngsters in the throes of choosing a career. That in this new guise the medical man was the dashing protagonist who "gets the girl" in plays, films, and popular stories would have been sufficient enticement for many of us. But there was more. There was the glaring prowess of medical advances. For the first time in history, the means became available to control infectious diseases, which until then were notoriously desperate; likewise, drugs were introduced in the fifties that could, beyond any doubt and for the first time, arrest the progress of forms of cancer that had been uniformly fatal. The physician ceased being the ridiculous personage exploited as a cliché of comedy. He became the shaman, the thaumaturge, to whose esoteric knowledge and magical potions the suffering world could address its imploring appeals.

The surgeon's stance was raised even more spectacularly. Improvements in anesthesia and general nursing care permitted him to manipulate the most delicate of bodily structures: the brain, the eye, the heart, the great vessels—all the tissues and structures that were deemed "noble" or so critical to life that interruption of their function, even momentarily, was bound to cause death. For the image of a barber-surgeon, who rashly attempted bloody procedures akin to butchery and whose unfeeling coarseness earned him mocking names on the stage—"Doctor Fillgrave," "Professor Sawbones," "Doctor Kill'am," and the like—was substituted the hieratic, majestic figure of a priest of some esoteric, secret cult. To restore the lost health of a sick person, this high priest would perform a solemn ceremony during which, as Paul Valéry saw it, the body of the sufferer was lowered into a magic dream, then slit open by white-gowned, gloved, whispering initiates who penetrated its interior and worked diligently with their own hands (for this, to work with one's own hands, is the pristine, etymological sense of the word "surgery") in its most recondite recesses, "under a crystal sun."

Such magical powers we wished to seize ourselves. The secrets of this miraculous cult we wanted to possess. For we knew that with this knowledge came also the approbation of society. Whether, or how much, the reality differed from our youthful idea was something we never paused to consider. It did not completely escape us that there were limitations in the idealized picture that we traced of our chosen field. But we were young, and therefore unmindful of such things as might discourage action. Overflowing with energy and enthusiasm, the young are ever ready to tackle the boldest projects. Brashness thrives with detriment to calculation. Because the young minimize wariness and circumspection, it is they who accomplish feats worthy of being recorded in heroic gest. Or, if a different expression is preferred, youth undertakes so much *because* it knows so little.

Descriptions of the trials and tribulations annexed to medical studies are legion. A scholar a few years ago, critical of the proliferation of these narratives, wrote, in a certain tone of irritation, that there appears to be no end to the public's taste for memoirs and personal recapitulations of the rigors experienced by physicians in training, first in medical school and later during the harsh initiation rites of hospital internship and residency. It is my intention not to contribute to the genre but only to relate personal experiences that, to my eye, had an unparalleled cast, and certain episodes which left an indelible impression upon me.

It would be hard to imagine a more awe-inspiring setting for a medical school than the building that housed it in Mexico City in the early fifties, shortly before it was moved to a new, architecturally spectacular university campus. Some medical schools may justly claim a more venerable history. Others, no doubt, better facilities, a more competent teaching staff, better equipment, or more illustrious alumni. But if there is such a thing as a suprasensible presence; a "spirit of the place," such as the Oriental fancy proposes; a lingering, invisible trace of the lives that were before us in the world—if such a composite phantasm somehow abides in the stones of an old building, then the old medical school of Mexico City was to be ranked with the gravest and most formidable of constructions. For that building had been the headquarters of the Holy Inquisition during the time of the Spanish colony.

Everywhere in their imperial possessions the Spaniards of the sixteenth century built structures to last forever. And everywhere they raised churches of massive dimensions, as if to anchor firmly in the heart of the lands they conquered the Catholic orthodoxy they so fervidly championed. So it is that the medical school building, originally an ecclesiastical edifice, was flanked by the Church of Saint Dominic, in the plaza of the same name, and was not far from many other, minor temples. The constructions were dirty, or in woeful disrepair, but it did not require too great a strain of the imagination, upon looking at the hoary stones, the massive wooden doors, the colored tiles representing pious scenes, and the niches for statues of saints at the corners, to fancy oneself transported several centuries back, to the time of the Spanish crown's rule.

Not having been raised a practicing Catholic, and professing my own youthful version of agnosticism, I never thought to visit the interior of the Church of Saint Dominic until I saw it praised in a popular magazine as a jewel of colonial architecture. One summer day, in the blinding glare of high noon, impelled by curiosity, I went in. It took a long time for my eyes to grow accustomed to the dim twilight that reigned there. No valuable art treasures were to be found in the nave's enclosure. A sickly, stale, unpleasant mustiness and a sense of oppressive desuetude, heavy with the scent of incense, suffused the air. In a corner, enveloped in deep shade, the silhouette of an old woman kneeling beside an image of the Virgin Mary; and down the aisle, by the flickering light of densely arrayed votive candles, barely discernible under the shadow cast by the fret of screenwork, the outline of a young man sitting quietly, in meditation or prayer; otherwise, the church was quite empty. On the main altar, beside the Queen of Heaven, was a statue of Dominic himself, Don Domingo de Guzmán, the holy man from Castile who wanted to evangelize the Tartars but was ordered by Pope Innocent III to go preach instead to the Albigensians in France's Languedoc.

Not eager to prolong my stay inside that dank, oppressive precinct, I quickly toured the nave and advanced toward the exit. It seemed to me then that the man I had vaguely seen sitting on a bench, absorbed in his thoughts, was my classmate, Hector Durán. The idea of someone leaving the school at midday, to sit down, alone, in quiet collectedness, inside an old church, was utterly puzzling. Only a few old women, and a rare

old man, attended that place. As far as I could tell, my classmates were a rowdy bunch; none could be expected to manifest religious leanings. Least of all Hector Durán, the only son
of a rather well-to-do family, whom I considered a superficial,
bourgeois "daddy's boy," whose whole background, radically
different from mine, served to dissociate him from the more
"proletarian" circle I frequented. He was older than the rest of
us, his classmates, by at least five years. This alone distanced him
somewhat from the group. And he lived in a fashionable sub-
urb, in a *garçonnière* such as none of us could afford, which he
had shared transitorily with another student at the beginning
of the year. He could draw important sums of money from a
bank account that his father, an industrialist residing in a
northern city, had set up in his name. The act of visiting a
church, in itself banal, so grossly conflicted with the idea I had
made to myself of the character and disposition of my fellow
students, and of Durán in particular, that I felt I had to come
closer to the visitor, to make sure I had identified him cor-
rectly.

I was momentarily stopped by the sight of a statue of
Christ carrying the cross, kept inside a large glass cage. It was,
to put it succinctly, a typical Spanish Christ. Not the gentle
Redeemer casting a glance of supreme wisdom and divine
compassion upon the disconsolate human race, but the other
one, the Son of God who chose to incarnate as a man—*Ecce
Homo*—and, having assumed this flesh-and-blood condition,
was mocked, vilified, humiliated, flagellated, spat upon, and
crowned with thorns. The loose hairs streamed down, largely
hiding the face, sticky with gore; the flanks were bruised; and
every laceration, ulcer, abrasion, sore, and swelling was rendered with gripping, painful realism. Yes, although now natu-
ralized Mexican, this Christ loudly proclaimed its Spanishness

in its very excess and in its gruesomeness. It used to pass for truth (or so Théophile Gautier claimed, and I will not presume to deny it) that the loincloth around a statue of Christ on the cross in the cathedral of Burgos was made of human skin. "O Spain," wrote Galdós in an oft-quoted paragraph of his *Episodios Nacionales*, ". . . there is no disguise to cover thee, no mask to hide thy face, no fard to disfigure thee, for wherever thou appearest, thou art recognized at once from a hundred miles away: one half thy face fiesta, and the other, misery; one half bearing laurels, and the other scratching leprous sores."

I was absorbed in these musings when the young man I was trying to identify scurried out the door. I could not be sure he was my classmate; the scanty light in the temple, and his wearing dark glasses, obscured his facial features. I tried to follow him, without success. Stepping into the street, I was blinded by a sudden flood of intense sunlight. It did not take long for my eyes to adjust, but the man was nowhere to be seen.

Earlier that day, back in the school, an unforgettable, shocking spectacle had presented itself to our sight. The venerable, three-story edifice was disposed, like so many Spanish colonial buildings, around central quadrangular patios. On each story, a corridor that bordered the central patio allowed the students to circulate freely and to access the various classrooms, which opened directly to this passage. And on the side of the corridor that faced the patio, a series of arches supported by columns and joined by an ornate balustrade added a graceful note to the otherwise stern, imposing gray stone structure. Between classes, students leaned on the columns and balustrades and tarried on the corridors, chatting idly.

Suddenly, a deafening roar, a tumultuous, loud din, such as I had not heard before in that hoary building, reverberated against the walls. It arose from hundreds of students who crowded the corridors on every floor, all looking down intently, whistling, screaming, tapping on their books, and trying somehow to increase the noise that broke out abruptly, like a thunderstorm on a summer sky. I ran to see the cause of the clamorous racket and wedged myself into an observation post against the balustrade. Traversing the patio were two janitors, each man carrying a large wooden plank on his back, which was steadied by means of belts passed around the shoulders and across the forehead; and on each plank lay a male human corpse, a semimummified naked cadaver, itself carefully fastened to the plank with strong ties.

Words cannot adequately describe the dreamlike, surreal aura of this scene. It is not enough to point out the strangeness of the spectacle: two dead human beings, undignifiedly transported, in broad daylight, on the back of menials, as if on beasts of burden. Nor does it suffice, to convey the nightmarish quality of the sight, to say that with each step of the porters, the inert bodies bobbed up and down, rhythmically. One of the corpses, his arm loose, appeared, with every step of his bearer, to wave at the crowd of excited students who watched him, ululating, from corridors set at three different levels, as from the tiers of a stony amphitheater that might have been dreamed up by Piranesi. But none of these details helps to reconstruct the sensation of the unreality, the mystery, of that scene. It is still necessary to add that all this was happening in an old building where one could see sculpted armorial bearings above the lintels, and reliefs where one could descry the broad-brimmed, tasseled hat symbolic of the cardinal's dignity conferred by a pope; and stately halls with tall beamed ceilings, beneath which secret consistories had once taken place; and dark back rooms with immensely thick walls, where those accused of heresy who had not abjured were brought to trial without right of counsel; and still darker, more ominous corners, where heretics who did not recant and were adjudicated civil as well as spiritual rebels collapsed, white as a sheet and covered by cold sweat, under the cruelest tortures that fanatical, pitiless men had devised.

Why were the bodies transported in such a shameful way? The explanation I heard later was that these were "unclaimed bodies" donated to the medical school—that is, cadavers of unidentified individuals found dead on the street, then kept at the city morgue for a long time, without friends or relatives ever coming to retrieve the remains for burial or other appropriate disposal. Most were homeless indigents, derelicts who had succumbed to disease, urban crime, or drug abuse. The law allowed that these corpses be turned over to the medical school for anatomical dissection. In itself, this practice was not unusual. In the Western world, since the late-medieval period, those most apt to end up on the dissection table were the poor: indigents, beggars, executed criminals, or unidentified persons who had died away from home. As to the offensive, painfully indecorous manner of the transport, the reasons put forth were strictly technical: that the school was in the process of moving to the new campus; that the equipment and personnel ordinarily in charge of this function were unavailable, on account of the transfer; and that transporters from the city morgue, unfamiliar with the proper procedures, had been in charge of carrying the bodies. But none of these reasons satisfactorily explained the odd scene, or the sense of acute uneasiness, of unyielding despair, and of fiery revolt that attended it, impelling hundreds of students to howl, to yell savagely, as if to exorcise the resistless evil forces triggered by the public defilement of two dead bodies.

For this alone seemed clear—and many of us perceived the concreteness of this knowledge for the first time: that we are utterly impotent before the powers of Nature. We were young, therefore unlikely to believe in the good of renunciation. Our hearts were buoyant with hope, overflowing with desires. But the two cadavers, out in the noonday brightness, hauntingly foreshadowed the ruin of all our hopes and all our yearnings. We were eager, spirited, sensuous. But here, before us, was the concretized image of body as waste, as despicable object, as the abode of impurity. The Buddhist texts emphasize the weakness of the body: it is fragile, like a jar; and in death it shall lie inside the earth, forgotten or despised, "without understanding, like a useless log." In meditation, the ascetics teach, the image of the body as a "corpse eaten by worms" is to be kept constantly before the mind. It was out of disgust with the body and its limitations that Gautama went forth from a comfortable domestic life into somber mystical reflection and the religious life. But we were no mystics, those of us gathered that day in the former seat of the Spanish Inquisition. Therefore, our response to the sudden vision that the body is a sphere of suffering was simply to scream. Two corpses, lying on respective slabs, silently addressed us, and told us: "You, too, shall go this way. At first, you are to lose your dearest. And soon enough, as the wave of destruction rolls on relentlessly, it will be your turn to enter the realm of darkness." And our sole response to this solemn, terrible, unspoken formulation was to scream, and yell, and slam our books against the balustrade.

On the other hand, we shared the equally distinct intuition that not all is somberness in the body. Every beat of our young hearts carried this intimate persuasion. It was materially impossible for us to dwell on lugubrious thoughts. Gautama, who taught that release from suffering is possible only through emancipation from the body and matter, also taught that the body should be cared for, good habits inculcated, and suicide forbidden. Our own Judeo-Christian tradition contained much to exalt the worth and dignity of the body. That the Son of God elected to become man, in the Incarnation, does away at once and completely with any idea that there is something essentially evil or degrading in possessing a perishable body.

Therefore, the agitation subsided. Silence was reinstated in the shady patios of the venerable building. The cadavers were deposited in the anatomy department's refrigerator. No one spoke of the strange scene, in which we had been the spontaneous, unrehearsed actors. Classes resumed, and no morbid thoughts recurred in our minds.

That evening, shortly before the activities of the day were suspended, lists were posted with the names of students who were to perform anatomical dissections on the newly arrived cadavers. Teams were formed. I was to dissect the superficial muscles of the posterior aspect of the leg; the deeper region was assigned to Hector Durán, the student whose putative presence in the church had so intrigued me.

No sooner had I identified my name on the lists than I realized Durán was behind me: the same person, I now confirmed, whom I had spotted in the temple. I said to him: "It looks like we are on the same team." He looked at me blankly and answered nothing. But he had removed his dark glasses in order to read the lists. And I noted that his eyes were much reddened, as if with crying.

Had Durán been crying in the church? To all appearances he had an inner life, and a troubled one, I thought. Had I mistaken Durán for a superficial playboy, when he was actually a sensitive young man in prey to some spiritual crisis? That day, the thought of our impending first direct contact with cadavers had been lurking in the students' minds. Was this the source of Durán's weariness, the sudden realization that man is, as the Stoics phrased it, "but a soul carrying a corpse"? Had he felt, only more strongly than any of us, how brief and powerless is our life, how pitilessly doom falls on everyone? For a moment, I fancied that Hector Durán might be as sensitive as the noble Yasa, of whom an old Sanskrit chronicle says that he left his palace because, after seeing the female musicians asleep, he could not repulse the stubborn mental image that "it was a cemetery he had fallen into."

In reality, the concerns that had driven Hector Durán to distraction were very far from spiritual crises or metaphysical preoccupations. He was in distress, no doubt. But the nature of his troubles was considerably more mundane, as I found out not long thereafter.

VIII

The Body of
Knowledge

———

*O*nce again, I peek into the dark box, the *camera obscura* of memory (is it inevitable to think of memory as file cabinet, chest of drawers, or other container? computers have yet to displace bins from our subconscious), and see two different pictures. My young self appears in one; the other is a classical painting viewed in a museum. One is a photograph, with no regard to artistic composition and symmetry, the other a magnificent work of art of an eximious painter. Why the two were filed together makes no sense, except that memory must be regulated by principles alien to aesthetics. The instantaneous photograph, somewhat yellowed and dilapidated, is of greater interest to me, on account of its personal, documentary value. Thus I will undertake its description first, in a spirit as candorous and uncompromising as that of its making.

The personages are all male students. Not more than half

a dozen: the number is uncertain, the picture being blurred from having been stored too long. The focal point around which they have gathered—we have gathered, since I can see myself on the left side of the picture—is a table, on which lie thick medical textbooks. The books are in complete disarray, most of them open, often one on top of the other. On the exposed pages one sees, here and there, the admirable detailed renderings with which artists illustrated anatomical descriptions in the tradition of superb craftsmanship that originated with Vesalius. Gray's *Anatomy* is there, ponderous and stuffy, like some English country attorney out of a Hogarth print; but most others are French: Rouvière, Testut-Latarjet, and others, just as massive as their English counterpart. These learned, serious preceptors are gathered here not to develop our reasoning faculty, nor to enhance our judgment, nor even to perfect our powers of observation. Their sole purpose is to transmit to us the impressive farrago of descriptive facts with which their thick frames literally burst at the seams. To this effect we plow into their interior, over and over, and reiterate the readings in an almost ritualistic way, as the faithful do with prayers that must be memorized.

But since what must be memorized is an enormous moiety, the effort must be steady, unflagging, assiduous to the point of self-mortification. First, we have recourse to the superb plates, wherein anonymous models are posing as flayed men, *écorchés* or *scorticatti,* whose skin and superficial soft tissues, previously incised, are pulled apart by means of metal hooklets. No one is holding these hooklets: in the pictures, they float unassisted in the air, yet perform their separatory function admirably well, so that the deep structures are displayed to great advantage, almost elegantly, enhanced by a rim of retracted skin. One might say that the body's insides are a theatrical tableau framed by velvety curtains, which are pulled apart with hooks that fold or indent the fabric at the point of insertion. The gaze then discovers a busy scenario: a devilishly complex system of interconnecting fleshy tubes, cables, wires, pipes, membranes, beams, pillars, receptacles, bags, bellows, pumps, and so on—all set on theatrical conventions that date we know not since when. For instance, the color coding is invariant: the veins are blue; the arteries crimson red; the nerves light yellow; the bones gray: the muscles brown. Not that realism is intended, since these hues do not correspond to those in the objective world. But the convention must be adhered to.

Next, we have recourse to all the mnemotechnical devices that ancients and moderns dreamed up. To remember names, series, items, relationships, we associate them mentally with numbers, or "sites and images" as Quintillian advised, or anagrams, or couplets, or whatever strikes us as expedient. Thus the ligaments of the knee joint are AEPI: the *a*nterior runs *ex*teriorly, the *p*osterior *i*nternally. Likewise, there are muscular regions, arterial branches, nerve radicles whose individual compositions are resolved into mysterious initials that sound like incantations: TROTA, DAMMI, REGEE. Enough cabalistic utterances that, had we ever repeated them all in a series, without pausing to breathe, there is little question that the Evil One, the Enemy of the Human Race, would have been conjured, or exorcised, as with AROINT THEE.

We also seek help from actual specimens. In the blurry picture, real human bones rest on the table and on the shelves. A lumbar vertebra, some students seem to think, makes an excellent paperweight. Others push their swagger farther and have improvised an inkwell from a scapula, a pencil holder from an ethmoid bone. But this cynical rashness, this defiant, sacrilegial temerity, is only a pose: such desk items are never used, for inwardly the would-be users are very much afraid of handling real human spoils. And there is, of course, the obligatory human skull: gaping, hollow orbits; unchanging wide-toothed smile; and smooth, clean, desiccated cranial vault, underneath which no thought has sparkled, no emotion been kindled, for many years. The ritual we engage in is to bounce from the text to the image, from the text to the specimen, from the specimen to the text, and from the image to the text. And again, and again: *once more, with feeling*.

The body grows numb, the mind weary, and the eyelids feel immensely heavy. And this explains why, in the picture, receding a bit away from the first plane, one of the students sleeps blissfully, his cheek resting on his forearm, while a trickle of saliva oozes from the corner of his mouth. It also explains why there is on the floor a basin with water and ice cubes in it, for the young man who is second from the right in the picture to plunge his bare feet into when he feels he is about to be overcome by slumber. A wake-up method that he finds preferable, he says, to the use of analeptics, a bottle of which is seen near the edge of the table, close to the pot of the concentrated coffee with which the tablets are swallowed. Guaranteed to keep you wide awake, on your feet, keen, alert. The state of mind that is indispensable if, at this late hour, one is to repeat, once more, the ritual of passage from the text to the image to the specimen. And all over again. And once more, with feeling.

The ritual is interrupted by conversation, perhaps once too often. For what purpose? To quiz each other with such questions as what are the branches of the external carotid artery, proceeding from up down or from down up. To defy anyone present, in a challenging tone, to recite the topographical relationships of the medial lemniscus as seen in consecutive cross sections of the medulla oblongata and the pons.

To sow the seeds of collective anxiety and confusion by stating that all this is a waste of time, that more time should be spent on memorizing the biochemistry of gluconeogenesis, enzymatic step by enzymatic step. To remember that the last exam was a disaster, a massacre, a veritable killing field. And to distract the collective attention with tales of levity, and ribaldry, and bawdiness, from the dreary repetition and mulling of the factual information that must be crammed. To the least sanguine among us, this abrupt change of pace is welcome; this brusque switch from force-feeding discipline to wild unrestraint is like coming up for air after a prolonged submersion.

For most of us, perhaps owing to traditional education, the idea of Woman is largely mythified. Woman is an alien creature, belonging in a different sphere, an altogether different world. Vague, ineffable, at once unreachable and inscrutable. She is a being that we perceive as superior in indeterminate, inexpressible ways. Her world harbors, in its deepest core, the fountainhead of maternal love, tenderness, charity, and such chthonic, fundamental warmth as makes life possible for humans and transmutes and inspires the Self. Women, individually considered, may be found wanting; nonetheless they remain creatures of an ideal world, largely unaccessible to men. Theirs is a world ardently longed for and often consciously renounced, a world whose gyrations always end up throwing men into a confusing ambivalence. Hence our inability to relate to women as freely, as frankly, as transparently, as to male friends. And hence our fascination with all this talk of bawds and meretricious sex.

A minute ago, our minds were filled with images of body as mechanism. Suddenly, they overflow with representations of body as source of pleasure. Most participants in the conversation are inexperienced, but those who have tales to tell hold the audience in suspension. What they have to say is as real as it is incredible, as commonplace and well-known as it is astounding and incomprehensible. That brutal hardships foisted on women by society should impel them to sell their bodies for money was not only cruel and shameful but essentially absurd. But, still greater absurdity, prostitution seemed attractive precisely on account of its ruthlessness and irrationality. That a woman should agree to go to bed with a man she has never known or even seen before; that she should, in exchange for a previously agreed upon sum of money, allow him the greatest of intimacies, the physical enjoyment of her body; that she should engage with him in deviant sexual practices, even revoltingly obscene ones, if the fee was sufficiently high—such trivial facts of common experience seem incredible and should naturally lead as much to disbelief as to outrage and rebellion. Yet there was no outrage, no rebellion. These facts, contrary to all dignity, actually sparked desire in the customer. That this desire existed in alloy with perversity was clear, since at its source was the ruthless pleasure of power, the enjoyment of seeing a young woman submit meekly to the man's whims, as a slave lowered herself to the commands of a satrap. But here again, reality dissolved into fantasy, or at least acquired the unpredictability of fantasy. These women, who must have experienced various degrees of disgust, patient resignation, or the sense of their own pitiless degradation, could act in perfectly natural ways, as if they were in the most normal of situations, playful, laughing, teasing, faking the spasms of sexual pleasure, with at most the ill-dissimulated indication that they wanted to finish fast. Enough to persuade the client, who by definition was enthralled by illusion at the outset, that there was not the slightest trace of aversion, revulsion, or sense of sacrifice in the services he received.

Those who have been there can explain to the rest how things actually happen. It helps, to enable the absurdity to take place, that the girls adopt a special garb. Nothing like clothes to mark distinctions, and distinctions are of the essence in this case. In war, a soldier might hesitate before pulling the trigger if a man clad in civil clothes appears straight before his rifle sight. Such a man could be anyone: a friend, a brother, a neutral individual; one who, in his general lineaments, in the vagueness of his nondescript clothing, would differ but little from himself. Therefore, a fleeting instant of doubt, or of self-justification, must precede the act of pulling the trigger. But if the potential target happens to wear a uniform, no hesitation intervenes: he is an enemy and is to be brought down automatically, without second thoughts. It is much the same with the girls in a cheap brothel. Their dress is characteristic. Some appear almost naked. Through a tenuous, transparent nightgown, the breasts, the outline of the nipples, the patch of pubic hair, show through. Or they wear stridently vulgar outfits: brassieres and panties with ribbons, bows, little tassels, and large, gaudily outlined perforations that expose what these clothes habitually cover. But that is precisely the point: these garments are not clothes in the ordinary sense of this word. They are not nightgowns, slips, or brassieres, however much they resemble those items. They are the uniform of the trade. In their terrible taste, their kitschy design, and their gaudy, vulgar ornaments resides an unmistakable distinctiveness. So that the customer feels at once separated from the woman.

And the woman, likewise, feels separated from the customer. She will not establish any form of rapport, apart from the commercial, with clients. Her uniform will remind her of her distinctive identity. A man may, on occasion, feel curious about her person and ask questions, usually the same: how long is it that she had practiced this occupation, how did she end up doing what she does, is she married, does she have children, what are the strangest requests she recollects from her customers. But to all this there will be the oft-rehearsed, indefinite, stereotyped, vague, untruthful answers. Sharing anything private is out of the question. The relationship is rigorously confined to the bodily plane.

Out of these impressions grew our youthful propensity to bisect the image of Woman. The split was down the middle: saint or sinner. She was either sublime in her matchless elevation or abject in her depravity. And through a tortuous train of thought, one whose sinuosities now seem easier to discern, I came to store the second picture, the artistic image, in immediate propinquity with the first.

The painting I think of is Titian's *The Two Venuses*. It is a striking composition, in which a wide rectangular easel appears as if divided in two by differences in light and color. On one side sits a richly attired lady, the very personification of elegance in her silks and jewels. At the opposite end of the painting stands a beautiful woman, almost naked, who completes the symmetry of the work. Between the two, though closer to the first one, is a fountain, on whose edge leans a Cupid, who playfully watches the rippling water. This painting is rich in Neoplatonic symbolism. Exegetes tell us that the two women represent the two goddesses of love, actually twins—*geminae Veneres*—of which one was known as the "celestial" Venus, Αφροδιτη Ουρανία, daughter of Uranus (but born of no mother, since the word *mater* is associated with the word "matter," and she was quite removed from anything material); and the other as the "vulgar" Venus, Αφροδιτη πανδεμος, daughter of Zeus (Jupiter) and Dione (Juno), who symbolized a concretized form of primordial beauty. Thus

the two female figures are the incarnation of the two pristine ideas—archetypes—of Woman that have existed for
thousands of years in the minds of men in every society.

However, it would be wrong to believe that what is expressed in Titian's painting is the simple opposition between
carnal desire and spiritual love. Actually, to the Neoplatonist
thinkers of the Renaissance, both Venuses were, as Marsilio Fi-
cino put it, equally "honorable and praiseworthy." The "vulgar
Venus" was not really vulgar: she was quite ethereal, albeit less
exalted than her "celestial" counterpart; her role was to stim-
ulate men's imagination and to enhance their sense perception
of beauty, not their sensual pleasure. In fact, contrary to what
we might expect today, the richly attired lady in the painting
is the "vulgar," or "terrestrial," Venus, whereas the naked female is the "celestial" Venus. This is in keeping with the Renaissance ideas of purity and innocence, which were often
represented by disrobed figures—in the iconography of the
time, "Justice" and "Truth" are scantily clad—whereas dis-
sembling and vanity wore ornate and complex robes, the better to hide their true colors.

Quite apart from these airy conceptions of the female
essence, however, there is obsessive sexual love. Neoplatonists
in the Renaissance would not dignify this condition with the
name of "love." Still, they acknowledged its existence, as had
the ancients, who coined the term *Hereos* to denote it. Neoplatonists considered it a disease, a form of mental derange-
ment. Its effects were much to be feared, like those of any
serious malady. When they condescended to grant it the name
of "love," they did so with a qualification: it was "bestial" love,
amor ferinus. Pico della Mirandola acknowledged the existence
of three Venuses, not just two, to accommodate the ruling
queen of "bestial" love. Her reality became clear to us upon

our confirming the sad experience of our classmate Hector Durán.

Hector Durán's brush with the Venus that presides over *amor ferinus* had a simple beginning. He did not patronize those cheap establishments that we talked about. At a party, he had been informed by one of his father's business associates, well into his cups, of the select circles in the world of prostitution. He was shown a business card that read "Jacqueline. Swedish, French, Middle Eastern & Asian Imports" and had a telephone number. And when he called, the madam, who had a foreign accent that he found impossible to characterize, expertly quizzed him on how he had found out the existence of her "boutique," and only after she was satisfied that the caller was an acceptable prospective client did she condescend to "set up an appointment" to show him some of the "products now in stock."

Hector went alone, his heart beating fast in the elation of anticipation, to the appointment in one of the finest residential districts of the city. The house was in a cul-de-sac, a little out of the way. Hector was a bit apprehensive, and but for the fact that there was still some daylight, he would have been downright frightened when a man opened the door. However, no sooner had he begun to try to explain his visit than a feminine voice from inside the house was heard:

"Marcos, it's all right. The gentleman has an appointment. Show him inside."

Hector was taken into a reception hall furnished in relatively good taste, if somewhat overemphatic in its allusive touches: on the wall, a mediocre painting of a rotund, pink-fleshed maiden, lying prone on a sofa, echoing Boucher; drapes in crimson velvet that effectively muted sounds; and a rather tall ceiling from which hung a baroquely ornate chandelier.

Jacqueline greeted Hector and for a moment seemed surprised at finding him so young. Clearly, she was used to a mature clientele: businessmen, politicians, foreign investors, men whose average age doubled that of the newcomer. However, her experience in assessing men's purchasing power was unmatched, and she soon appraised the young customer for what he was, namely the pampered son of a rich family. She led him across a corridor that overlooked a garden with plantain trees and a pretty fountain, barely distinguishable in the dying day, into what seemed a separate, two-story wing of the house. The chamber they went into was labeled "Testing Room" with a conspicuous sign in Bakelite. Evidently, despite the fact that prostitution was tolerated, the madam was careful to disguise the nature of her business with the trappings of a business of *haute couture.*

In the "testing room," three chairs faced a curtain and a wooden dais, raised about ten centimeters from the ground. One might have said it was a tiny theater. Hector and the madam sat down, the third seat remained empty. The curtains were parted, and three young women successively emerged, clad in suggestive lingerie. The first one was rather short and stout, and the very white rotundities of her generous frame appeared to be restrained with difficulty by the set of bands, crossing straps, and taut garters of her provocative attire. Surfeit was her ostensible, for-sale commodity: she probably catered to men with a penchant for excess. The second woman appeared just minutes after the first had paraded her trembling, overflowing charms. Although probably in her early or mid thirties, she looked forty, perhaps on account of a certain air of pervasive melancholy that effused from her person, and of deep, shaded circles around her eyes, which imparted to her mien a Baudelairean aura of decadence. She held a lighted cigarette between the index and middle finger of her right hand and gyrated in the restricted space of the improvised platform in that "exhibition hall." She swiveled her hips not unlike a model walking down the runway in a fashion show, but a look of supreme boredom in her eyes somehow undid, in a single stroke, the sapiently calculated sensuousness of her motions and the patiently contrived sex appeal of her dishabille.

The third woman, who made her stage entrance while the madam asked the young man whether "there was anything to his liking in what he had seen," turned out to be the prettiest. She could not have been older than eighteen or nineteen years of age. Youth, undoubtedly, was the primary source of her radiance. But there was also a boldness in her manner, a forceful, animal quality that went beyond the self-confidence of youth. One might have said it was the defiant attitude of a being who had been formerly hurt but has presently recovered and rises anew, borne aloft by a hubris that is part pride and part hostile desire of revenge.

This brazen, hardened look was very much on her face when she realized that Hector could not take his eyes off her. He was as if mesmerized in contemplation of her largely exposed body. Not that she was especially beautiful. Her breasts were smallish, her torso was short, somehow out of harmony with the rest of her frame, and her mouth was a bit too large, guarded by pulpy, protruding lips. But when she moved she appeared to betray an inner tension and a sinewy elegance that were almost feline; and her carriage transpired a self-assurance that, by dint of imperious gestures, kept Hector Durán constantly in prey to an invincible fascination. A fascination that he would have been at a loss to explain.

It sometimes happens that the ineffable power that one

being exerts over another is immediately perceived by the dominant member of the pair. The girl was alive to the fact that from her body issued forth a kind of energy that intromitted directly into the young customer, who experienced it like an electrical charge. Without changing her pace, with the same bold demeanor she had exhibited all along, she walked straight up to him, seized him by a wrist, and said while looking brazenly into his eyes: "Well? Shall we go?"

The madam smiled broadly and remarked: "It seems, sir, that your choice is made." It would have been more accurate to say, "You have been chosen." And she added, slyly: "You may go upstairs with her. If you wish, that is . . ."

Without releasing him from her grasp, the girl conducted him to a bedroom up one flight of stairs. As Hector reminisced later on, very few phrases were exchanged at the time. He asked her name and heard her say it was Victoria and that everyone called her Vicky. Her surname? Sellerio. "An Italian name," she noted. And without much further ado, as casual phrases were still being bandied, she sat on the edge of the bed, removed one by one the few undergarments she was wearing, arranged them carefully on top of a chair nearby, and hopped under the bedsheets. Then she said: "Well, what are you waiting for? Come on, get over here! It's darn cold here, you know. . . ."

Hector undressed, joined her under the sheets, and was enveloped in her warm embrace. He felt her body pressed tightly against his, and it seemed to him that his limbs weakened and something at the core of his being slowly deliquesced; as if his central sustaining axis became atomized and dispersed in an all-enclosing wave, where he was being tossed here and there, at random. She grabbed his face with her two hands and kissed him on the mouth with a kiss that was fundamentally professional, although it may—dispensing with overly rigid criteria of authenticity and taking into consideration its duration and the exploratory movements of the tongue—have passed for passionate. Hector felt as if cut off from the world of everyday reality and hurled into another dimension, of which his recollection would be, in the long run, not as vivid as that of the preceding moments.

And that was all. It was as simple as that.

On the Might of the Vulgar Venus

———

*A*t first, he did not think of her. Young, affluent, and moving among the rich and idle, he felt quite confident—this, by the way, justifiedly—that it would not be too difficult for him to procure himself any kind of female companionship, whether mercenary or otherwise, if the whim assailed him. It was not immediately apparent to him how deep an impress she had wrought on his psyche. When he surprised himself thinking of her, he quickly dismissed this mental activity as insignificant. However, the recurrence was unexplainable. "That girl has something," he said to himself, taking refuge in a *non sequitur*. And that was all: he was inclined neither to brood nor to search for explanations where the most cursory initial survey had uncovered none. "She has something," he repeated, and did not think of her any more. Happy are those who, in the face of things perplexing, mysterious, and terrible, find solace in a word! To them, the word is what a pacifier is to nursing babes: they suck on it until they lull themselves back to their usual slumber. "She has something!" End of disquieting enigmas.

And so for a couple of weeks her image did not irrupt into his brain. He was called home by his father during a school break. But once he was in his homestead, a ranch just outside a provincial, sleepy town, the days grew long. His father had urged him to come back in the name of family togetherness, a value he professed to hold sacred: "You must come more often. After all, this is where you belong. Here, with your own kind..." Empty protestations, Hector knew full well. He had not been there two days when his father was called away by an important business transaction in Houston, Texas. Nor was this unusual. For as long as he could remember, it had been like that: a father ready to extol the supremacy of family values but never there; who sang the praises of tradition and stability but kept a common-law wife, as was widely known in the town. "Your place is with us. Your sister is growing into a fine-looking young lady, and you hardly know her. Come back." But now that he was back, he found that the little sister had returned to Quebec, to continue her schooling with the nuns, and would not be back for six months. Surely his father knew it. His peroration on fraternal love had been, as usual, strictly rhetorical.

As to his mother, she was caught in a dense web of pious, church-related activities. She went from rosary to novena, to retreat, to charity function, to spiritual exercises. Long ago, she had ceased to have eyes for the things of this world. Or ears, for that matter. Life's asperities she successfully avoided by absconding to a world of litanies, rogations, hymns, and reiterative confessions. Let someone tell her that her husband was disloyal: formerly, she would have groveled under a pain greater than she could bear; today, she was perhaps grateful for having something to add in her prayers to Judas Taddeus. She was no sage, obviously. She had not painfully ascended the steep path that leads to tranquillity of spirit. She had merely blinded herself in a cloud of incense; deafened herself with a rumor of prayers. She did not detachedly contemplate the world: she deliberately ignored it. Should someone dare to confront her with the reality that injustice, misery, and violent passions were afoot in the world, she would retort with a high-pitched "Holy Jesus, Mary, and Joseph!" that was simultaneously an interjection, an invocation, and a jussive stop to the conversation. How would Hector be able to talk to her?

Hence her son became restless. His childhood friends bored him immensely. He and they had grown mutually apart. Still, with the best of intentions he sat with them long hours in a sidewalk café on the central plaza, forcing himself to follow their tales of local fairs, horses, and fights and scandals in nearby towns. The conversation then turned to handguns. An interminable discussion followed concerning the relative virtues of the pistols they possessed. Someone said that he owned a German nine-millimeter Luger and that up to the time of its production, this was the most powerful handgun built. Someone else disagreed, vaunting instead the Colt forty-five. To Hector's dismay, this conversation lingered on for the better part of an hour. Some affirmed that a projectile from a Luger pistol, when shot from a certain distance, could perforate a rail of the railroad track that passed through the town. Others denied this assertion. The Colt owner was challenged to pit his weapon in competition against the German Luger; bets were placed, and a contest began to take form.

The utterances of his friends began to sound ever more remote in Hector's ears. Suddenly, across the plaza, he caught sight of a young woman who walked of a brisk pace. He felt absolutely sure that she was Vicky: the same protruding, fleshy lips, vaguely adumbrated in profile before she turned into a lateral street; the same elastic long legs; the same hairdo, with the hair collected in a small chignon at the nape. He left precipitously, barely excusing himself, to run after the young woman. However, when he got to the street corner where she had turned, he found the place deserted. He walked up and down the street, lingering awhile in front of open doorways and peeking inside. But there was no one to be seen.

As soon as he returned to the city, Hector Durán telephoned Jacqueline's "fashion business," for a tryst with Vicky. On the appointed day, his heartbeat was running fast even as he approached the house. He was ushered directly into a room where Vicky was already waiting for him. She greeted him with a "Hello, darling" that caused him great disappointment. It felt like a cold shower. That "darling" was dropped with such vulgar affectation and in such tone of voice as to sound like the typical salutation of a professional call girl.

He asked her whether she had been recently in his hometown.

"Me? In my life I never set foot in that dump."

"Are you sure?"

"Of course I'm sure. Why would I lie?

"No, I just thought I had seen you there."

"No way. You've got me mixed up with someone else."

"What's wrong with going to visit that town?"

"It's a dump, I tell you. I've got no business there."

"But you *could* go there if, by some accident, it happened to be your birthplace. . . ."

"I was born here. And my mom's family, thank God, is from G———."

"So you don't think it a disgrace to go to G——?"

"I go there from time to time. When I get offers for a job..."

"You mean at houses in G—— like Madame Jacqueline's house?"

A sudden flash of anger glimmered in her pupils, and her features hardened as she retorted:

"Because you think I cannot do any kind of decent job?"

"Well, I didn't say that. I meant..."

"You meant I am just a whore, good only to be jumped on in bed?"

"No, of course not. I didn't mean that at all. I... I..."

"For your information, I have worked for a couple of years in an advertising agency. They have a branch in G——. They call me now and then, and sometimes I do work for them here as well. But to you, a whore is just a whore. Something to be used in bed, not quite a human being."

"Okay, okay. You made your point. I apologize. I didn't mean to offend you. Don't take it so badly...."

"I don't like people prying into my affairs, anyway. So cut it out. Enough said."

As she spoke, she removed her dress, then her undergarments, and without transition, in a scolding tone, she said to him: "Come help me undo my bra." She sounded as if she were still arguing with him. He obeyed, meekly. Then, with imperious gestures, from which the signs of irritation had not entirely vanished, she pulled him toward the bed.

Lovemaking that evening was altogether bureaucratic— two commissioned employees executing a task overseen by the business administration.

But who can fathom the absurdities ensconced in the human heart? Experiences of this sort, fit to cut short the progress

of erotic passion—nay, to squelch it into outright extinction—
worked precisely the opposite effect in the young man. The
more such squalid, depressing incidents took place, the fonder
of her he appeared to grow. He returned to her again and again,
trying to find out more about her without much success.

"Where do you live?"

"I don't give my address to anyone."

"At least your telephone number. Maybe I can call you
once in a while and we can meet somewhere else, not in this
house."

"I don't have a telephone."

"Then how come Madame Jacqueline can call you?"

"She doesn't call me. I call her."

"What's wrong with telling me where you live? You know
me well enough to know that you can trust me."

"There are things I tell to no one. To no one, you hear?
That's the way it is. Some things are best kept private. I don't
like people messing around with my stuff, you know?"

And her facial features seemed to turn rigid, somber, tense
with anger, so that he did not dare to continue the questioning.

For him, the recurrent cycles of desire and satiety took on
a strange, obsessive character. It seemed right to speak of an ad-
diction, so sharp was the compelling urgency of his desire.
Soon his infatuation could not be concealed. The madam
smiled slyly at his eagerness, anticipated his demands, and skill-
fully manipulated him into spending money for drinks, gifts,
and various expressions of unaccustomed largesse.

By assiduity and perseverance, he obtained to meet her
outside the brothel a few times. The rendezvous were always
on her terms, and never at her place, whose location he continued in ignorance of for many months. Often, these meet-

ings only increased his frustration. Sex was not always the end point of these encounters. She would ask to be taken to a show, to a nightclub, to a friend's house. Not uncommonly, a male friend would pick her up to drive her home. Hector remained behind, prey to jealousy, anxiety, despair, and humiliation. But also fear. Fear of not seeing her again, and this alone held in check his wrathful impulses.

It must be owned that he was no stranger to his predicament. "Caught by a little whore!" he said to himself, reproachfully. "How could this happen to me?" And in a moment of lucidity, he reflected that the whole affair was ridiculous, pathetic, plainly stupid. It was the typical trap about which stories abounded: the traditional snare in which simpletons from the countryside, such as the ranchers around his hometown, became entangled. All the more absurd that this should happen to him: young, traveled, educated, and with money at his disposal. Certainly, he could have other women: prettier, kinder, more honest, and, in sum, worthier of his affection than this one. Therefore, he tried to rebel against what he perceived as a humiliating bondage.

On one occasion, when Vicky failed to come to a prearranged assignation, the madam suggested that he take with him another girl, Pamela. Several women present exchanged a look of intelligence that cut him to the quick. In reaction, he faked nonchalance and indifference: "Sure, it's all the same to me." But when he was alone with Pamela in the bedroom, he felt confused and utterly discouraged.

Matters were made worse by Pamela's malicious teasing: "Sneaky little creatures, aren't we? That one doesn't come, and right away we're unfaithful. . . ." Hector blushed to his ears in embarrassment and anger. He was mad at himself, for being so weak, and so transparent to others. But, curiously, he was also angry at Pamela, for having referred to her, to Vicky, as "that one," an expression implying a contemptuous familiarity. This language amalgamated the two women into one somehow, placed them on a plane of perfect equality. Consequently, he thought, Vicky was brought down to the same level as the pitiful, vulgar strumpet now standing before him. And such were the irrational, disordered notions filling Hector's mind that he could not suffer this idea. For although the objective evidence showed that Vicky was, undeniably, a colleague of the prostitute who now addressed him, yet in his mind she stood immeasurably above her level, so high above her vile stance as to make it a gross impropriety, almost an indecency, to refer to her in terms of such disrespectful chumminess.

His discomfort was only made worse by the studied maliciousness of Pamela, who toyed with him:

"You're really very, very fond of her, aren't you?"

"She pleases me, that's all."

"As far as I know, you're her first steady customer. Before you, none of the men she went with ever came back for more. I bet they didn't appreciate the tricks she does. . . . Some, I suppose, may have been disgusted, although with you men, one never knows. . . ."

"Really? What does she do?" asked Hector, intrigued and shaken.

"You know . . . ," she answered slyly, looking at him from the corner of her eye, while she removed her clothes. "Dirty stuff."

He felt his limbs weaken, and his mouth went dry. Still, he retorted trying to master his emotion: "I don't understand. Please tell me. What are you saying?"

"You mean you don't know? I can't believe *that one*

didn't do it with you! It's her specialty, you know, which she must have perfected after trying it with so many..."

He felt his strength abandon him, while a diffuse sense of anguish progressively took hold of his entire being. In a hollow voice, he echoed her last words, mechanically: "...with so many..."

Unaware of his growing despair, Pamela kept teasing him: "Many? Thousands! *That one* must have done the whole police department, let me tell you...."

Intensely pale, with greatly altered mien, raising his voice almost to the point of screaming, Hector exclaimed, imploringly: "For God's sake, stop it! I beg of you: tell me what she did with so many! I have to know!"

Pamela was taken aback by the violence of his reaction. She recoiled and uttered an apologetic retraction. "Take it easy ... I was just kidding."

But Hector had risen, trembling, undone. Putting on his jacket, he was seemingly on the verge of tears. He threw a roll of bills onto the night table and with an irate gesture rushed out the door, while the girl, not quite recovered from her surprise, exclaimed: "Hey! Wait a minute! Where are you going? I was just kidding. Come back! Can't you take a joke?"

It was not until he reached his apartment that Hector gave free rein to his emotion. Sitting on the edge of the bed, his elbows on his knees and his face covered by his hands, he let go his tears in a free flow, punctuated by short saccadic tremors, sole accompaniment to his muted, almost inaudible sobs. Those were sobs of pain and of rage: a rage directed mostly at himself, for being so stupid, for having fallen head over heels for a juvenile slut, a doll-like, impudent hussy who could be had—whom *any man* could have—for a fistful of money. And his despair deepened upon his considering that he could expect no sympathy; that indeed he deserved none. His friends, if he were to tell them how he felt, would rightfully brand him an idiot, a moron; and he would be the first to agree that the label was just. His parents, what would they say? How would his father anathematize him? As for his mother, she would pray to God, no doubt. And in the present circumstance, perhaps that was the only sensible thing to do. For he was like a man possessed; like one visited by an incubus. An incubus in the shape of a young girl.

He now realized that to try to cast off his chains was futile. Work, school, distractions, duties, and varied interests: nothing could reverse his enslavement. For every person, every activity, every attempt to read or to occupy his mind, ended up reminding him of Vicky Sellerio. And every face, every image, and every situation, by tortuous routes, through unexpected associations of ideas, or by oblique, sometimes bizarre lines of reference, ended up converging , unfailingly, in the evocation of her person. Contrariwise, such things as failed to advert to her presence appeared to him nonexistent or drained of meaning. Medical studies, family, friends, plans for his future: none of these things seemed to matter. Indeed, the whole physical world was to him phantasmagorical: buildings, roads, boats, cars, rivers, were like cardboard semblances, since they had no connection with her. And the women, the countless women who lived in the world, and among whom there were undoubtedly millions upon millions of young girls prettier than Vicky, more sensual than Vicky, kinder, worthier, more sensible . . . what could they possibly matter to him when only one—she, and only she—could abate the growing, unremitting fire that devoured him?

It was the day after the distressing incident with Pamela

that I spotted Hector in the nave of Saint Dominic's Church. Perhaps he was not quite recovered from his agitation, and the idea had come to him to collect his thoughts in the temple, before appearing at school. His attendance, it goes without saying, had become quite irregular. His morbid obsession, and the canvassing of its associated misery, utterly filled his mind. He was like a patient with an abscess or some other painful tumefaction, grievously suffering on its account but finding I know not what perverse pleasure in palpating it, feeling it, and pressing upon it with his own hands, that a soreness be triggered at will—a pain made sharp or dull under the control of his own fingers.

The third Venus, she who presides over *amor ferinus* and truly deserves the name "vulgar," subjugated Hector Durán. Wild deity that she is, she tortured him savagely and unremittingly on the rack of jealousy. It was she who planted in his brain the idea to offer financial assistance to Vicky, if only she would quit working in the brothel and spend more time with him. Hector told her he would take care of her housing expenses and provide her, additionally, with a living allowance, not to mention the outlays for entertainment that he was habitually contributing already. In exchange, she was to make herself available to him in less restricted fashion than theretofore. The poor young man did not aspire to exclusivity of enjoyment—he was not so blind. But he was reduced to such an extremity that he did not mind paying for extending the time that she would be with him. Payment, after all, had been established from the start as a feature of the relationship. Therefore, the new arrangement seemed natural: it would be like an extension of the terms that were customary. She would consent to accompany him on pleasure trips. He would have freedom to visit her, under certain conditions, in her apartment.

It was not exactly monogamy, what he was proposing. But he realized he would become, *de facto,* "official lover"; and since he would be footing the bills, he expected to have at least some of the prerogatives annexed to such a title. Vicky also understood the implications of the arrangement. She would be the "kept woman," a role for which society has long decreed specific, although unwritten, advantages and limitations. She listened attentively to the young man's halting exposition: how he had access to substantial funds that had been set aside in his name and would allow him to keep his promises; how these funds, representing a minimal part of his father's business ventures, would not be missed for a long time; how she would live free of worries if she accepted.

Much to his surprise, she did accept. Not without conditions, however. She would not give him a key to her apartment. He would never appear at her place unannounced; it was understood that he did "not own" her. But she agreed to see him more often and more freely, and to frequent Madame Jacqueline's "boutique" no longer.

After Durán entered this arrangement, we saw him less and less. His scholastic record had been borderline; it was now a complete debacle. How did he live in those days? What went through his head? Was he so utterly besotted by his infatuation as to leave no room for anything else? He had no close friends, but classmates who had more than a casual acquaintance with him reported having met him while on an outing, in a night-club, with his girlfriend. Allegedly, he had manifested that he intended to "take some time off" but would return to school after a while. His dependency had become so serious that sex no longer seemed the primary reason for his bondage. Whoever had been capable of looking inside him would have seen this. But in the most widespread opinion among us, his peers, he was a prisoner of his own base impulses, a serf of the sovereign power of sex: a thralldom that moralists would unanimously deem contemptible, for a self-respecting man should live for more than the genital urge. "Larger am I, and created for a larger destiny, than to be a servant of my body" (*Major sum et ad maiora genitus, quam um mancipium sim mei corporis*), wrote Seneca with his customary grandiloquence, in an epistle to Lucillus (65.21). But the stark fact is that Seneca's grand-sounding pronouncements had absolutely no echo with us. To our eyes, Hector Durán was a winner, a favorite of Fortune: wiser in the ways of the world than any of us and envied by us all, almost without exception.

The rumor spread like fire among his former classmates: Hector Durán kept a woman—a prostitute or an ex-prostitute—as his mistress. Only what a prostitute! Certainly not the pitiable wreck that preachers had in mind when they sermonized on "vessels of sin"; not the grotesquely painted streetwalker who looks like a repository of abjection, depravity, self-abasement, and every manner of physical dilapidation and moral aberrancy. But neither was she the splendiferous courtesan, the beauteous woman of the world, seductress of kings and rich nabobs. She was simply a pretty young girl: she looked like a vivacious college student from the middle class. Hence her subtle, unopposable seduction. When Cato, the ancient Roman poet, advised his son to "shun a harlot"—*meretricem fuge*—it was implied that the counseled would know exactly what to flee from. Vicky Sellerio did not differ in appearance from many young girls with whom Hector Durán had been acquainted. Clad in fine clothes, she looked fresh, sprightly, like the fiancée of one of Hector's classmates. He could think of her as having brothers, a father much like his own father, even a boyfriend apt to give her an engagement ring and wait for the banns to be published at the local church before taking her to bed.

But this was only an illusion, a hellish form of *trompe l'oeil*. For this young girl, graceful and comely, could be had for money. All that was needed—and this was almost incredible, an immensely astonishing fact—was a certain sum, not all that inaccessible.

Hector Durán, though older than his classmates by only a few years, surpassed them all in worldly sophistication and financial ease. Thus they easily raised him to the rank of the enviable. He had it all, and now had a beautiful concubine too, like an Oriental potentate. But the truth is that unbeknownst to all, including himself, he entered his very own Dolorous Chamber, the seat of his most harrowing pathos.

Jealousy was the first cause of his suffering. She saw him more often, but he was never sure whence she came and whither she was going. They went together to Acapulco, Cancún, and Miami. At each of these places she seemed to know the fanciest hotels, the most fashionable bars, on occasion even the personnel. When had she been there before? With whom had she come? And Hector could not stop thinking that she had stayed in the same hotel, possibly in the same room ("Come, come, Hector, let me show you the fantastic marble bath they have upstairs . . ."), with another man. Who? Some middle-aged, paunchy, bald politician, or some mumbling, sniveling old financier, or perhaps some swinish, sweaty, uncouth rancher. Any of the men she might have met at Jacqueline's.

Predictably, Hector would choke and ask Vicky if she had stayed at the same hotel before, and with whom. And he would get all manner of answers and find none of them satisfactory. Then he would press the questioning, never being able to catch her in a contradiction. In the end, he would sound recriminatory, and the conversation became uncomfortable:

"How come you ended up working for Jacqueline? You don't belong there."

"I've told you a thousand times, I needed the money...."

"But you could have worked. You could have found a regular job."

"Oh, yes! I saw it coming! I saw it coming!" And sarcastically, imitating his utterance: "'You could have been a secretary, like one of those nice girls who work in my daddy's company. But instead you chose to be a whore. A whore! A whore!' That's what you wanted to tell me from the beginning, isn't it? Well, I don't have to take this from you. You don't own me. I don't take this kind of shit from no one...."

Tremulous, she would put on the clothes she had removed and begin getting her things in order, arranging her baggage, as if preparing to leave. And Hector would calm her down, and appear humble and contrite, until she was persuaded to stay.

The unreflective, apt to judge from purely external, objective occurrences, made the facile conclusion that Vicky was what is popularly called a *femme fatale*, the heartless exploiter of men who, like a man-eating harpy, enjoyed sucking the blood of her victims bone dry. But she was no more a bloodsucking monster than Zola's *Nana* was a preternatural demon or Merimée's Carmen a creature from hell. These personages of fiction, like the flesh-and-blood women unfortunate enough to raise a like reputation, are perhaps insensitive and irresponsible, but they remain profoundly human. Yet it is plain that they are easier to demonize than to understand.

What thoughts could possibly arise in the brain of a little girl who was a prostitute in a brothel? Did she become nauseated at the moral squalor and universal pollution of her environment? Did she feel disgust at the beastliness of men, at the obscenity of their requests? Dismay at their hypocrisy? Sadness at the abjection she saw herself fallen into? Resignation to her own misery? Strange to tell, it seems to me that none of these applies. Nausea, disgust, dismay, sadness, and resignation are dark animic states. They thrive in decaying ambiences, not in the airy, luminous childish heart. And Vicky Sellerio's heart and mind had all the potencies and all the limitations of immaturity. She was incapable of dwelling in those dark sentiments for any length of time. Nor was she capable of seeing that their inception is, under some circumstances, an absolute moral imperative.

Prostitution, to her, was a challenging game. A vertiginous, sometimes exhilarating, dangerous game, like gambling or drug usage. Not that she found in it any physical pleasure. The reward of the game was money, not sensuality. But she did derive a bizarre form of pleasure, akin to that produced by flattery: a strange sense of proud satisfaction upon corroborating her power over men. Young and old alike, they responded to her body: dazzled by its youth, swayed by its radiance.

Durán told her that he loved her. In token of his protestations he set forth impressive deeds of magnanimity and forbearance. One might have been easily convinced that love, and love alone, could prompt so much patience and generous detachment. But was it really love? After all, he never offered to marry her. What would his parents say? Deep inside, he trusted that once the first boiling of his passion was spent, he could do without her and return to "normal" life. Only the first flame was not easily extinguished. It became, instead, an ungovernable conflagration. And the more he thirsted after her, the more diffident she became. Hence a vicious circle was started: he pressed her to return his professed affection; she retorted with reaffirmations of her independence and with behavior that made him jealous; he swallowed the humiliation with alacrity, out of I know not what masochistic relish, and renewed his protestations; this led to new rebuffs, destructive of his dignity. Until, one day, he became pathologically depressed.

They were in a mountain resort not far from the city. In a restaurant, they encountered an old acquaintance of Vicky's, who occupied a table with several other persons. The man was David Zales, a television executive. He and Vicky shared much familiarity, judging from the friendliness of the mutual salutations. Zales asked them to join him and his party at table, but she declined, saying: "I don't want to interfere with your plans, since it appears that you've finished eating. Besides, you and I would only be talking business, and Hector would be terribly bored." Then, addressing Hector: "I tell you what. Please go to the bar and get a table. I just need to talk a few minutes with David. I'll join you in a minute."

But she did not come for close to an hour, to Hector's unalloyed dismay. When she finally appeared, she announced startling plans. Zales had offered her the opportunity she always wanted, to work in the television industry. The fortuitous encounter had been a stroke of luck. Zales said he had been trying to contact her but could not, since she had moved to a new apartment. As it turned out, he and his crew were on their way to the town of T—— and had stopped for lunch. If she could accompany them, Zales offered to use her as a model in a commercial. They would shoot some footage of her, to be shown to the sponsors. This might be her lucky break. And she was so elated and bubbly that Hector, despite his frustration, did not find the courage to protest. She reassured him further, saying: "I will only stay there tonight. You could, if you wish, come to pick me up tomorrow, say, at noon. T—— is only a two-hour drive from here. It's on the highway that leads to your hometown, I believe...."

Hector was disarmed. And she added, in a sweet tone: "I'll leave you my suitcase and my topcoat. T—— is at the foot of the mountain, and the weather is much warmer here. I won't be needing the coat. I'll take only my handbag, with a few personal items, all I need to stay overnight. Take care of my things, will you?" And she left him behind, once more prey to the green-eyed demon of jealousy.

Who was this Zales? What sort of relationship did he have with her? Hector reflected that Zales was a mature man, perhaps in his early forties, at the peak of his career, vigorous, and clearly an appreciator of feminine charms. Modishly attired, with a dash of ostentation, surely he was an influential don in show business. Hector, in contrast, was a boyish-looking young man who must have seemed awkward. Was he playing the fool for them? They were so familiar, greeting each other with kisses on the cheeks! Perhaps at this very minute they were laughing at him! Perhaps merely to recapitulate his infatuation gave them the giggles. "He is the one who pays!" she would say. And he would add some scurrilous remarks that would make the whole company explode with laughter.

But wait! They had not all gone together. She climbed into Zales's car, but didn't the rest of the crew get into a different vehicle? The two of them, alone in the car... He could picture her childish insouciance, and her devilish, seemingly guileless coquetry, laden with those gestures of the false ingenue. He imagined how she would sit in the car by the man's side, oblivious to the fact that her skirt had insensibly been raised, exposing her thighs. Or perhaps it was with a studied air of artlessness that she exposed herself, as when she grasped her skirt with both hands and agitated it up and down with fanning motions, presumably because she wished to relieve the heat she felt but in reality to show her legs. And the man, what would he do? Desire could be so easily sparked! He would want to possess her right then and there: "Not here, David, for goodness' sake—you're going to wrinkle my dress! Wait until we check in. . . ." Surely he would wish to possess her, without really bothering to think much about her, either before or after the sexual act. Whereas he, Hector, really loved her! Why did she refuse to see that?

He looked at her suitcase and at the coat she had left with him, one minute seized with wrath, wishing to tear the garment to pieces and throw the suitcase into the fire, and the next minute embracing the coat lovingly, as if she were inside it, and looking at the suitcase with a glance of tenderness, because it represented a sort of guarantee that he would see her again, that she would come back to him.

Spurred on by these thoughts, he decided to drive to the town of T—— that same afternoon, in search of her. On the road, the lance of jealousy did not relent in its ferocious thrusts at his heart. He imagined his sudden arrival at the hotel. The clerk would stop him at the registration desk. She would be forewarned and come down to meet him in a hurry. She would detain him, while Zales, who surely would be in her room and in her bed, would have time to get up, dress, and come downstairs to greet him, as if nothing had happened. And the two would be laughing at him behind his back. . . .

Then, as he drove his car in the direction of T——, something unexpected and most remarkable happened; something altogether unexplainable. His jealousy abated, and a different sentiment, profoundly depressing, replaced the fury of his passion. No sooner had the town of T—— adumbrated itself in the distance than everything began appearing to him as senseless. Not merely his present situation, but everything: his morbid attachment to Vicky, his past life, his projects, school, friends, family. Everything seemed purposeless, fake, a big charade. In the depth of his suffering, where all his thoughts seemed nebulous, as if enveloped in a mist, only this idea emerged distinct and plain as daylight: the idea of universal meaninglessness. He did not stop at T—— but kept driving, toward his hometown.

As the pure light of happy love is said to provoke supreme revelations otherwise inaccessible, so the lurid flashes of tormented love and sickly passion have their own revelatory powers, by which human beings may discover the darkest aspects of life. So it is that Hector's unhappy love thrust him squarely in front of the "barbarous teaching of reason," as Leopardi called it, namely the intimate conviction that all human pleasures and pains are but deceits and that only the certainty of the nothingness of things, or the works that derive from this certainty, can be deemed just and truthful. "And if by adjusting all our lives to the sentiment of nothingness," wrote Leopardi, "our world comes to an end, and appropriately we should be deemed crazy, nonetheless it remains formally true that this would be a reasonable craziness under any aspect, so that compared to it all wisdom would be craziness, *because everything in this world is done by the continuous and simple forgetfulness of this universal truth, that all is nothingness.*"

Hector Durán had journeyed through scholastic failure, exasperated eroticism, thwarted desire, exploitation, misery, and furious jealousy. Through this circuitous route he had reached existential anguish, the *maladie du siècle*, the disease the ancients called *aegritudo* and Petrarch and his contemporaries named *accidia*. Despair. Universal hopelessness. One injury is not enough to inflict it. But the cumulative effect of severe blows, and the addition of boredom and disenchantment, succeed in bringing it about. This feeling, that life and human undertakings are all pointless, is like a lethal shadow that sterilizes all virtues and blights the best fruits of the mind. Cicero recognized it for what it is, "the source and beginning of every sadness"—*in ea est enim fons miserarium et caput (Tusc.* 4.38.83).

He was not expected at home. With his friends, in the sidewalk café, he managed to maintain an outwardly tranquil demeanor. He did not appear too bored during the long discussion, renewed in deference to his presence, on the relative merits of various handguns. His mother came back from a church gathering, effusively greeted him, and soon retired for the night. He could not sleep. Such is the nature of *accidia, aegritudo,* or whichever name his malady may receive. Petrarch noted that while in other passions there is an admixture of sweetness, in this one all is rough, and painful, and horrible. The assaults of other passions are more or less transient, but the pressure of this one is constant, day and night.

The moon emitted a bright, eerie refulgence, and numerous stars dotted the night sky. Suddenly, an explosion reverberated in the house. Hector's mother sprang up from her bed, screaming, without quite knowing why. She came downstairs, where she saw the motionless body of her son. The upper half of his body sprawled awkwardly over the center table in the living room. One arm was caught under the torso and seemed twisted, the other hung pendulous. She shook this body, and turned it over, and saw a rivulet of blood streaming down the right temple, from a small hole that could be seen only with difficulty, because it was covered by hair.

A smallish hole, indeed, considering that the weapon, still on the floor, was reputed among his friends to be able to punch a hole through the steel rail of a train track.

X

Undocumented Alien in the Kingdom of Freedom

———

*W*here medical schools spend as much time and effort in systematically screening and rigorously selecting applicants as they do in English-speaking North America, it is taken for granted that all those admitted shall finish in due time. Thus students notified of admission have cause for celebration: official enrollment is tantamount to receiving a diploma a few years thence—barring, of course, serious illness, death, personal tragedy, or other *force majeure* causing the interruption of their studies. Where, in contrast, admission is lax, unrestricted, and informed by the populist notion that the liberal professions ought to be easily accessible to everyone, down to the humblest members of the least favored social classes, vast numbers of applicants are admitted, and precious few will graduate.

The differences are interesting, and possibly telling of the mind-set of those responsible for each system. In one, the student is treasured. He, or she, represents a carefully distilled, slowly perfected product: academically outstanding, technologically minded, especially proficient in those disciplines that form the basis of contemporary Western medicine; moreover, often the offspring of affluent parents, since tuition fees tend to be very high. Let such a student manifest signs of failure in any academic subject, and the most earnest, concerted effort of the faculty will be mobilized to remedy the deficiency: meetings will be convened, counseling may be provided, tutorial efforts implemented, and all sorts of remedial measures organized. This solicitude for the individual reflects the school's conviction that the student body is uniformly excellent, its members having been carefully selected for intellectual acquirements and personal aptitudes uniquely adapted to serve the medical profession.

The other system may be said to be essentially fatalistic. It starts out from the premise that in life, everyone eventually settles in his preappointed place, no matter how much agitation may be temporarily imparted to the circumjacent milieu. Thus are thousands admitted, since an opportunity must be liberally tendered to all, and only a limited number are expected to finish. Nor will the failure and frustration of so many disturb or incommode the professors. It is, after all, in the nature of things. So it is that the disappearance of Hector Durán went virtually unnoticed. He was only one among hordes of students who, hoisted by their own petards, were flunked, or academically deflated or exploded. No serious effort to find out what happened to him was made by the school; and since his death occurred some time after he had been away, he was not missed by the professors, who hardly knew him.

As to which of the two school systems is to be preferred, I should not wish to venture an opinion. The one has enviable

standards and consistently produces some of the world's outstanding figures of modern, scientific medicine. On the other
hand, it remains an elitist system, efforts toward democratiza-
tion notwithstanding. Individual attention to trainees, and
their adequate exposure to all the latest technological innovations in their field, is enormously expensive. In a capitalistic society, this tends to rule out a not inconsiderable number of
talented applicants unable to afford the cost of tuition and
whose personal circumstances disbar them from acquiring the
heavy loans that might make their schooling possible. Con-
versely, a few of those who manage to be admitted are unfit,
by reason of temperament, sensibility, or outlook on life, to engage in the practice of medicine. But they would not be dis-
suaded from an endeavor undertaken at so great a cost. Nor
would the faculty easily admit any responsibility for the wrong
choice, after a collective effort of the best educators was put
into the meticulous and much-vaunted selection process.

In the other system, money is no obstacle. But standards
are uneven. Since resources are scarce, and made even scantier
by the unmanageably large number of students, individual attention is unthinkable. The school authorities are unable to
evaluate thoroughly the fund of knowledge and the acquired
skills of the students. Hence the quality of the graduates is apt
to vary immensely, from some who would compare favorably
with the best anywhere in the world, to many dismal ignora-
muses, whose loosing upon society may be equated to foisting
the plague on a defenseless population. And since enforcement
of the standards of medical practice is ill-implemented, the
population may be said to be truly at the mercy of cunning
exploiters and skillful, ignorant dissemblers.

Yet learning, from both life and school, was still possible
in this disorganized, resource-poor milieu. It was possible to

learn medicine, as well as the dificult art of living. One had only to be attentive to the lesson. Life had used the cruel example of Hector Durán to illustrate how erotic passion, though outwardly delightful, manages to hide its train of woe. As the raw recruit desires to see combat and when blood and death finally appear is afraid and horrified, so do the young ardently desire *amor ferinus*, and often live to regret it. Had we been good learners, we might have understood the wisdom in the ancient saying "Only the inexperienced miss a war" (*dulce bellum inexpertis*). Or as Vegetius put it, in the only military treatise surviving from the time of the Roman empire,* "Distrust the raw recruit's desire for combat: strife pleases only those who haven't tasted it."

With regard to our technical preparation, it was evident to all of us that the outstanding physicians in the community, those with the most solid theoretical background and well-earned prestige, had obtained at least part of their training in the United States of America. This was the new Mecca of medicine, the place where modern Aesculapian votaries must go, as in olden days they repaired to Bologna, Paris, or Vienna, for ritual initiation, confirmation, and sanction of their status. And as the medieval pilgrims donned their broad hats, pinned a shell to their capes, grasped their walking staffs, and set out to the shrine of Compostela, so did I prepare my luggage and, in the company of a cohort of my comrades and with comparable fervor, make it north to the fabled land of America.

We had been hired as interns in a clinic in the state of Colorado. I went by bus: almost three full days of continuous grind.

---

* *Epitoma rei militaris* 3.13. A recent English translation of this text exists, entitled *Epitome of Military Science* (Philadelphia: University of Pennsylvania Press, 1996).

This took place in the sixties, when crossing the border into the United States of America could still strike the foreign traveler with a sense of wonder and a young man raised in a Mexican barrio could find plenty of motives for astonishment. The visible prowess of human industry left me speechless. Here were stupendous bridges thrown across immensely deep, wide canyons; smooth, broad, multilaned roads that coursed over the roughest, most ragged terrain; inhospitable deserts converted into pleasant greeneries; and those colossal dwellings, aptly called "skyscrapers," uprearing their gigantic, overwhelming masses. The splendor of constructions, the magnificence of public works, even in remote or relatively small towns, amply proclaimed that I had come to the most powerful nation on earth.

However, together with the excitement of gradually discovering all these portents, I felt some uneasiness. It was an undefinable mixture of uncertainty over my own future, worry at having to cope with unknown ways, and regret at leaving behind loves, familiar sights, and habits, which were, so to speak, the stays that propped my existence. Without these I felt unsupported, insecure, threatened, as I entered the new, unknown country. A foreign territory presents itself to the deeper zones of our consciousness as a land inhabited by "the Other"—i.e., those who are not *our* people. Mircea Eliade noted that such a land impresses our imagination as having "the fluid, larval modality of chaos."* The unknown country seems labyrinthine, dark. At a less arcane level, I was nostalgic for my family and my friends. For who is so unfeeling, or so unhappy, as not to love his native land? Even those wretches who were born in the most destitute corners of the world, if later they should

---

* *The Sacred and the Profane: The Nature of Religion* (New York: Harper & Row, 1961).

settle in more affluent regions, cannot help feeling nostalgic for the country of their birth. Lucian wrote that even "among men completely overmastered by the lust of the eye," none is found who would completely forget his homeland, just for having come across sumptuous riches elsewhere.*

Soon the contrasts between the country of my birth and that to which I had come waxed increasingly apparent. I was to reside in Colorado Springs, at the foot of Pikes Peak. Founded with a different name in the last century by a railroad entrepreneur, General William F. Palmer, this town was to become not only a stylish mountain resort but a settled area of considerable importance, in which several military installations are headquartered: the North American Air Defense Command, the Aerospace Defense Command, the Fourth Infantry Division, and the U.S. Air Force Academy. The latter, with its bold modern architectural design, offers an impressive sight and is still the place where the elite of the air force's officers are trained.

My first impressions of this beautiful town are still vivid in my mind. The snow-capped crests of Pikes Peak raised their haughty silhouette against a sky of pure azure. As I strolled through a residential district close to my workplace, I could hardly contain my admiration for the clean, orderly appearance of streets and dwellings. There was a neatly tended lawn fronting every handsome residence. The institutions of learning seemed very well provided for. The public buildings were excellently maintained, bespeaking the efficiency of the transactions that took place inside. But at the same time, I was seized by a feeling of strangeness at finding very few people in the

---

* "My Native Land," in Lucian, *Works*, vol. 1 (Cambridge, Mass.: Harvard University Press, 1991), p. 209.

streets. It was not too late in the evening; it could not have been later than five or six o'clock: the time when, in the barrio, the streets began to buzz with rapidly intensifying animation. Yet here it seemed as if it was past closing time and everyone had retired for the evening. I was sure I had arrived on a national holiday.

The next day, having installed myself in the room that the hospital authorities rented to me inside their institution, I went out to reconnoiter. Same solitude: only a rare human figure could be discerned in the deserted, windswept, silent streets. But the loneliness of the site was not the lugubrious loneliness of a "ghost town" or an abandoned settlement. The manicured lawns, recently painted facades, and prim hedges were too neat for that. All these details reflected the constant involvement of careful, industrious inhabitants. But where were they? My inquiries led nowhere. My coworkers said that I noticed little activity because I had just arrived from a large city and this, after all, was a much smaller town. Still, I knew that a town of comparable size in Mexico, nay, a town much smaller than this one, would display a much higher level of public activitiy.

At length, I understood that communal social activities entailing such displays as strolling aimlessly in the streets, sitting idly in the central square or its downtown equivalent, and standing around chatting and "killing time" were generally classified as dishonorable praxes. Order, cleanliness, and efficiency, I began to suspect, were acquired at a price.

I must reiterate that my impressions were gathered upon arriving in a rather small town. Life in the great cities of the United States, like New York, San Francisco, or Chicago, can be quite different. For this very reason, life in the large, cosmopolitan urban concentrations is often thought of as "unrepresentative" of American life.

The streets were deserted not because the population was scant but because local ways hindered walking and street assembly. The well-paved roads and broad streets had been designed not for idle perambulators but for the swift displacement of automobiles, of which almost every household had at least one. Social intercourse seemed limited to that possible on the job, during working hours. There seemed to be little opportunity, or inclination, for people to go sit together and talk in a café, or linger in the streets in amiable chitchat. After work, most people would get into their cars and drive over well-designed, well-maintained roads to a comfortable single-family house. The house (I was going to learn that the usual term in this context is "home") acquired a great importance, largely because in the realm of freedom, life is lived in interiors, since there is so little to foster an outside life.

Even in shabby residential districts, the houses had a front lawn and a backyard. It was refreshing to see that every house owner could aspire to live like the landed gentry. But to furnish each household with a parcel of land, no matter how small, meant to augment the distance between houses. Consequently, contacts between neighbors decreased, and dependency on the automobile increased. Did one need to buy an aspirin in the drugstore? Food in the market? Impossible, unless, of course, one went there by car. Repining from the difficulties in transportation—for of course I didn't own a car—I was reminded of the complaints of a sixteenth-century Spanish *hidalgo* when a horse-drawn carriage had just been introduced. The rich bourgeois who owned one, he said, spent their lives inside it and ended up resembling the tortoise, who carries her house on her back and sticks her head out only now and then, to see how the weather is outside. And the tirade finished with this uncharitable adjuration: "In their blessed carriages they shall be dragged to hell." Vaticination that, at the time, seemed to me applicable to a vast sector of the American citizenry.

When, in the barrio, my mother had the idea of buying a pair of shoes, she walked to the shoe store, where a minimum of fifteen minutes was spent in chitchat with the manager or the salesgirl, after which each party had a clear idea of the status of the other's family. If what she needed was to be found not in the neighborhood stores but in some more distant establishment, whose personnel was not of her acquaintance, approximately the same amount of time would be consumed in bargaining. The ancient art of bargaining affords, where it is duly practiced, an opportunity for becoming acquainted, since it demands an attentive assessment of the personality of the interlocutor. The transaction usually ended with the vendor making such a statement as: "Neither you nor I, dear lady. Let's make a deal and settle in the middle: eighty pesos." To which my mother would retort: "Sorry, sir. Seventy is all I have. Take it or leave it." And this peremptory assertion was accompanied by a move that indicated she was leaving. If the sale was to be completed, she would be recalled—retrieved, as it were, when already halfway out into the street.

In the country I had come to, the art of bargaining had been sacrificed to speed, efficiency, and profit. Prices were fixed. Chitchat with the customers was rare. If small talk was indulged in, it never reached the personal plane. In the neighborhood market, I never witnessed any haggling with the salespersons over the inalienable right of the buyer to test produce by squeezing it. Never did I hear the assertive vendor's warning often heard in Mexican markets: "If you don't buy 'em, don't bruise 'em" (*Si no compra no mallugue*). Instead, an attendant would place the goods in a bag, taking them from the pile at random, and a register would record the price. No chitchat. *Time is money.*

In my native country I was, not uncommonly, irked by the multitudinous character of certain aspects of daily life. I was irritated by uncouth crowds pressing upon me; dismayed by the chaotic, even riotous, jostling at places where orderly formation might have rendered life much easier for everyone. I was disgusted by the sweaty, unkempt, ill-smelling populace that congregated in public places or in buses and other conveyances. I avoided, if I could, the popular open markets, where the effluvia of sweaty bodies mingled with the emanations of spices, ripe fruits, and frying, greasy snacks from stands and eateries. And all this was joined to a loud din from vendors hawking their wares, and the haggling of customers and vendors, and radios playing at the top of their volume, and the not too harmonious sounds of the ragged minstrelsy that used to eke out a meager living in public places.

In my new country of residence, there was none of that; and this absence I experienced as a relief for some time. Soon, however, I missed the very things that formerly annoyed me. The realization dawned on me that those traits were but expressions of a pervasive desire for companionship, manifestations of the desire to seek out the presence of the Other. In a sense, the things that had bothered me so much could be compared to eddies in a muddy pond, visible from the surface as dirty turbulence but emanating from a hidden wellspring of brotherly love. For what common denominator can possibly underlie friendly chitchat, bargaining, haggling, and even arguing or fighting, if not a lively interest focused upon the Other? Wrangling and conflict are undesirable by-products. But at least their origin can be traced to an interest in human interaction that is close to love. That the opposite of love is not hate is well-known: it is indifference. The kind of indifference—ever more prevalent in industrialized societies—shown by strangers who walk into the same elevator and for a few seconds share the same reduced space without crossing a word and without establishing any other rapport than that of a mutual sly, precautionary glance, to avert danger. The kind of indifference masterfully captured in a scene of Federico Fellini's film *8½*, in which rows of automobiles stop in a traffic jam and the drivers in neighboring lanes look at each other from behind their car windows with absent glances or with a gaze that seems at once frowning and unfocused, indifferent, irritated, and distracted: the gaze of a man who is thinking of something other than what he sees.

In a very entertaining book, the Italian writer Luciano De Crescenzo developed the idea that there are places ruled by the sign of love, and others ruled by the sign of freedom.* Where love is dominant, daily life is characterized by frequent interactions among people and intense emotional interdependence. Here, however, individual freedom is severely curtailed. The "kingdom of love," as De Crescenzo calls it, extends through several countries, without regard for current geopolitical divisions; its dominion includes primarily southern countries, but not exclusively so: Ireland, for instance, and parts of Russia are included, in spite of their northern location. Typically, however, the kingdom of love is climatically warm; for life takes place largely in the open, a circumstance favored by pleasant weather. Each individual's joys, fears, hopes, misfortunes, triumphs, shames, defeats, tragedies, aspirations, illnesses, and

---

* *Così Parlò Bella Vista: Napoli, Amore e Libertà* (Milan: A. Mondadori, 1977).

victories are known by everyone: they are, like most of life, "in the public domain."

Of course, in such a place, it is well-nigh impossible to have any privacy. Friends and visitors drop in unannounced. The constant noise perturbs. Reflection, quiet collectedness, and a peaceful inner life are highly prized, because rarer to acquire. In the populous neighborhoods of the "kingdom of love," such precious mental states can scarcely exist. They wither amidst the screams of neighbors arguing, spouses shouting, children bawling, and visitors irrupting when least expected. The longtime resident of the realm of love tends to adjust, and resigns himself to the prevailing limitations, but also suffers grievously under its maddening pressures. These are not easy to bear. The inhabitant of the "kingdom of love," even if native to those latitudes, sighs for a little individual freedom. Freedom from the relentless intrusion of others. Freedom to be by himself, able to meditate and to introspect and to find out how far he can develop his individual potentialities. But as soon as he finds himself transported to the "kingdom of freedom," he is unhappy. He feels a chill in his heart. He realizes how badly he needs the others. He will conclude that he is what he is largely through the others, and therefore he cannot be himself without them. And unless he is by temperament inclined to change his allegiance (for not everyone is attuned to the temper of his birthplace), he will yearn to return to his native grounds.

It has been remarked that the word "privacy" has no exact equivalent in the Romance languages. *Privacidad*, in Spanish, is a barbarism of recent coinage, taken directly from English; and *vida privada* corresponds to "private life," which means something quite different. By the same token, cognate terms such as French *intimité* or Italian *intimità* correspond, obviously, to "intimacy," whose connotation is not the same as "privacy." All of this points out that the Latin countries belong indisputably within the kingdom of love, whereas England and the countries of English tradition, including the United States, form a bloc that falls squarely within the kingdom of freedom. Few would quibble with the assertion that Italy is part of the kingdom of love, although some northern secessionists there might find fault in so including the totality of that country.

According to De Crescenzo, the capital of the kingdom of love is the city of Naples. Who does not know (at least through photographs, as I do) those narrow streets where lines that bear the laundry put out to dry in the sun connect the upper stories of buildings on opposite sides of the street? Those clothes and linen are the banners and standards of the capital of the kingdom of love. And the lines that bridge the streets are a symbol of the interconnectedness and close intertwining of the lives of the inhabitants. For indeed, merely to set those lines from balcony to balcony, spanning the street, implies neighborly concert, agreement in design, and more than casual mutual exchanges. Add to this crowded conditions, narrow streets, warm weather, the exuberance of Neapolitans, the openness of their lifestyle, and it will seem plausible to contend that Naples is the capital of the kingdom of love. De Crescenzo wrote that if Almighty God ever conceived the idea of fetching a Neapolitan house to heaven, a second building would soon follow, and then a third, until the whole of old Naples was pulled heavenward; for all the buildings are tied to each other by clotheslines, which form a web as intricate as the net of emotional ties that bonds Neapolitans to one another.

Perchance someone will object that these appreciations are superficial and that I mistakenly see psychological differences in what is only socioeconomic disparity. In other words, that Americans and Mexicans, or for that matter other third world peoples, are not really all that different; and that given comparable levels of affluence and industrialization, they would react similarly. With this proposition I cannot agree. I would argue the opposite. If, by an effort of the imagination, I were to suppose Mexico converted into a world power, possessed of great military might, the most advanced technology, and boundless financial reserves, I would still not be able to see its becoming identical to the United States. Unsuspected similarities would perhaps become apparent. But it is a safe wager that these two countries would remain distinct and often contrasting in their ways. There would still be profound differences in attitudes toward life and the world; in how people regard time, work, women, leisure, children, the elderly, religion, love, death—briefly, in those elements that conform a civilization.

As a newly arrived immigrant, I was forced to adjust to each difference. I can refer only to some early impressions. Religion, contrary to my expectations, had a much more conspicuous place in everyday life than I was used to. In the United States, the First Amendment of the Constitution guarantees freedom of religion; but this Constitution was written by "founding fathers" who were staunch believers, had nothing but reproof for irreligiosity, and might have felt inclined to punish atheists. To date, an acknowledged agnostic or overt atheist would not dream of becoming President. Religious leaders beam their messages through the mass media. Politicians publicly exhort to prayer. Bumper stickers proclaim "Jesus = Peace"; T-shirts bear inscriptions that say "Keep on Trustin'" and "Jesus Saves"; colorful pocket-sized plastic cards are mass produced that declare "Jesus Loves You." Indeed, every American carries in his pocket or wallet one or more copies of a religious message, the "In God we trust" that is inscribed on dollar bills.

Roaming the streets each time I had some leisure, I greatly admired the fine state of the church buildings. I was amazed by the multiplicity of denominations: Lutheran, Baptist, Methodist, Unitarian, Congregational, Pentecostal, Anglican, Episcopalian . . . Scarcely had I learned the names of the major churches, when new ones seemed to spring forth. "Para-churches" proliferated side by side with mainstream religions, almost vying with commercial brands in frequency. But regardless of the name, the dainty upkeep of the premises was agreeable to behold. Surrounded by smooth lawns, flower shrubs, and hedges, illuminated at night by artfully disposed floodlights, these gracious temples, often in the Gothic style, were immaculately maintained. Panels mounted outside the door announced the topic of the coming sermon, the schedule of services, and the name of the preacher—not unlike the way programs and show times are displayed by the ticket window in a theater.

To my surprise, every time that, impelled by curiosity, I tried to visit one of these churches, I found it closed. I was accustomed to expect the house of God to be open all the time, at least during waking hours. What if the faithful should be afflicted by a sudden spiritual crisis at, say, two o'clock in the afternoon? Should not the souls thus distressed flock to the temple for consolation at any time, as the bodily diseased run to the emergency room for urgent treatment day or night? Here, however, it was communion with the deity by appointment only. Or else spiritual intercourse with the Almighty took place in the *privacy* of the home, free from distraction. This was, after all, the realm of freedom.

When, at length, I saw the interior of a church, new

surprises awaited me. The services were all neatness, order, and civility. In Mexico's remote interior, I had seen sloe-eyed Indian women breast-feed their babies inside a temple and, at least once, a stray dog wander in—and it took his marking a column of the nave as his territory before anyone thought of chasing him. (It has been remarked that it is characteristic for precincts of public use in the "kingdom of love" to be suffused with a pervasive odor of human secretions. When animal excretions are joined to this scent, all but the most insensitive wish they lived in the "kingdom of freedom.") In America, the proceedings were characterized by supreme collectedness, cleanliness, and tranquillity. And so was the message. No theology of pain here. No gaunt, blood-spattered Spanish Christs. Instead, a Caucasian Jesus refulgent in a radiance of calm, soothing benevolence.

The building itself evinced further differences. The old churches of Mexico were built as native adaptations of the Spanish Baroque, whose extravagantly ornate modes the conquistadors successfully implanted. The complex decoration accorded well with men who were sentimental, violent, and of a morbid sensibility furnished with Arabic-Moorish undertones. Such men were prone to become absorbed in decoration for its own sake. Somerset Maugham, in his book *Don Fernando*, hypothesized that the exaggerated concern with decoration was a by-product of the repression exerted during the Counter-Reformation upon the minds of the artists, whose creative instinct was forced to conform to the dictates of the Church. Frustrated at not being able to paint what they really wanted, they turned to decoration—for lack of anything better to do, so to speak. Be that as it may, the result was striking: florid, showy, and eminently theatrical. In contrast, the temples I now could see in the United States were astoundingly bare of ornaments. And this was no fortuitous observation. Many American Catholics had rejected decoration since the turn of the century, on the grounds that it is distracting. Moreover, the use of complex ornaments was deemed a disease of artistic design: a cause of enfeeblement of architecture. Critics advocated the suppression of all ornaments, for the sake of expressing more forcefully the spiritual tendencies embodied by a temple. Examples of this architectural philosophy are the Church of Saint Francis de Sales in Muskegon, Michigan, and the Benedictine building in Collegeville, Minnesota. Both are austere constructions of bare, sleek walls and movingly simple, uncomplicated lines.*

The elevation of spirit that was pursued may be fostered by simple, abstract forms. But in the repudiation of realistic art, the walls were left sadly bare of paintings, as the altars were being left ever more destitute of sculptures and adornments. Opposition to realistic portrayals included representations of the Virgin Mary. A critic complained that inferior art often made Our Lady look like "a chorus girl with blond tresses." And a seminary professor, writing in a religious magazine, went so far as to suggest "simply to hire Peggy McGillicuddy, the charming president of the young ladies' sodality, to make a suitable custom, and stand on a pedestal over Our Lady's altar, with her eyes cast up to heaven."† One is to suppose the professor had some reason to impute high distracting potential to Miss McGillicuddy; how he came to think of her as a substitute for the celestial image is harder to explain.

---

* For a discussion of religious art styles in America, see Colleen McDannell, *Material Christianity: Religion and Popular Culture in America* (New Haven: Yale University Press, 1995), pp. 178 ff.

† Quoted in McDannell.

That Catholics resisted images of the Queen of Heaven was sufficient proof that the country I had come to was fundamentally different from the one I had left. Mexico was her dominion, where she had been raised to the rank of tutelary deity. Having acquired a skin the color of copper (from prolonged exposure to the sun), and thus resembling the natives, she was made their *de facto* national symbol. Her image was everywhere: from candy wrappers to altarpieces to banners. Historically, her image was known to appear on flags or regimental ensigns that were unfurled at the head of clashing armies on both sides. Therefore, imperviousness toward her image in America, like the diffidence regarding Mariolatry in general, struck me as a bizarre phenomenon.

In times past, the cult of the Virgin Mary did much to mollify the relations between the sexes. When the ideas of femininity and divinity were joined, the image of Woman gained a spiritual dimension it had lacked before and an ascendancy otherwise not easily attainable over men's consciousness. The suffering addressed to her, as celestial intercessor, their most desperate, heartfelt supplications. Hence the notions of benevolence and compassion were associated more closely with female nature; and this contributed to mitigate the harshness that men were prone to impart to their relationships with their natural companions.

There can be no doubt that the status of women in American society is immeasurably superior to that attained by women elsewhere. Although they must still contend with prejudice and discrimination, they have achieved equality with men before the law. They are protected from abuse and enjoy the same legal rights as men. They are free to engage in any honest occupation for which they are fit, even one traditionally considered masculine. They have achieved social and political gains that women in other countries envy and yearn for. Therefore, it seemed to me paradoxical that, even among Catholics, the Mother of God had fared worse than in less progressive lands. I wondered whether social and political gains failed to run apace with conquests of the minds and hearts; in other words, whether women's equality was legitimized by law before it had taken root in men's souls. This is the criticism of those who say that American women have largely achieved equality as citizens—i.e., as legal entities or subjects before the law—but not as women.

To grapple with perplexities such as these is called "adaptation." In the normal course of events, an immigrant is reconciled with new conditions. But the beginning is difficult, even traumatic, in the measure that the newly arrived is set in his ways. Like all immigrants, I felt at first very much like an outsider and gravitated preferentially toward the circle of compatriots—there is always "the community of exiles"—who were also my colleagues and coworkers. The community of exiles is what a biomedical term calls "immunologically privileged": it is insulated from the worst ills of the body politic. The convulsions of American society, its most grievous conflicts—there was a war in Vietnam, assassinations of political leaders, and a youths' revolution—we could still see from the outside, as foreigners who temporarily resided, but did not intend to settle, here. We were not indifferent or cynical; our status was that of sympathetic but aloof nonparticipants. And this status was natural to our migratory condition, as it was conferred upon us by the natives. The medical metaphor may be validly extended: the body politic rejected what it recognized as foreign.

On weekends, we used to gather in the home of a Mexican-American family, whose generous friendship eased our adaptation. Their house was away from the town, in a fruitful valley, surrounded by groves and cornfields that spread afar, unfenced. Many an afternoon found us picnicking in those verdant meads, and we might stay until late in the evening, gathered around a fire, eating roasted marshmallows and drinking pop or beer out of Styrofoam cups. One of the group strummed a guitar, and all of us sang airs of the old country, *corridos* (ballads) and popular romantic songs, mingling our voices to the sound of the wind.

When I evoke those days long past, the rustle of leaves is again in my ears, as when a rush of air came to stir the branches overhead. All around us, the evening began to descend, while gray mists rolled and stars on high flared one by one, like distant torches, until the sky became thickly sown with constellations. Then the sense of a fullness of life, possible yet still unrealized, came upon me and wrapped me in a reverie. Clearly I descried the ideal, bright promises of the future; its actual toils and pangs I met with a smile, incredulous. I was young. It was not pop or beer that I drank by those fireside gleams: it was life. For life was for us like a cup of frosted crystal, brimful of ice water, whose cool sweat we felt with febrile hands and anxiously approached to our lips. All of it we wished to imbibe: sipping not gradually but fast, and of a single trait.

Wild and uncontrollable is youth's thirst for life: it knows the good in waiting but is in haste to drink—so delicious seems the tantalizing freshness, and so burning is the thirst.

XI

There Is a World
Elsewhere

———

*I*t is over thirty years since I arrived as an immigrant in the United States. Yet it is still sweet to reminisce about that youthful enthusiasm for learning which induced me to leave my native soil. It was no less powerful than the impulse to escape the stultifying and humiliating constraints of economic neediness. My colleague friends and I knew that superb educational facilities existed where we were going; and I was determined to become more than an expert in a medical field: I dreamed of becoming a revered mentor, a sage. I realize now that love of learning was not so simple. I also hankered for economic independence, and recognition, praise, or honor. My motivation was less pure than conceit inclined me to believe. But I make no apology: on this score I resembled most men, who insist in calling their delusions, their varied forms of bondage, "glory," "love," "authority," "honor," and other high-sounding names. Petrarch hit the mark when he said that it is with us as with the man who, "tied down in shackles and manacles of gold, contentedly sees the gold, and does not see that it is chains" (*quam siquis aurem manicis atque compedibus tentus, aurum letus aspiceret, sed laueos non videret*).*

As to learning, over the years I developed a different attitude. I became convinced that it was important to rid my head of much of what had entered there from books. This process of disinstruction is most salutary; I heartily recommend it. It is akin to spring cleaning or rejuvenation treatments, and like these, it must be undertaken periodically for best results. Much that is in the mind is but a tangle of rusty and decaying concepts that must be thrown out without the least compunction. If in the process the valuable is thrown away with the worthless, it does not matter: the good in clearing the impenetrable morass outweighs the mischance of accidental losses. And then, absolute emptiness is preferable to mendacity. Otherwise, we end up convinced that we understand what we continue to ignore. Books breed this complacent belief, since often they persuade us that mysteries are explained away through recourse to other unexplained mysteries, the classical instance of *ignotum per ignotius*. Here I wish to retell one experience that shaped my distrust in the sovereign power of learning as an aid in the difficult art of living.

I was still an intern in a hospital in Colorado. We—a few former classmates and I—had been admitted to the lower rungs of the American system of postgraduate medical education. It was clearly a two-tiered system. On the top tier were graduates of American medical schools, most of them United

---

* Francesco Petrarca, *Secretum*, transl. into Italian as *Il Mio Segreto, La Letteratura Italiana: Storia e Testi*, vol. 7 (Milan: Riccardo Ricciardi, n.d.).

States citizens. They occupied the positions that offered the best educational opportunities in the foremost teaching hospitals of the nation. On the lower tier were those who, like us, had a foreign diploma and thus found it almost impossible to have access to these posts. We had to be content with jobs in community hospitals, where postgraduate education was comparatively inferior and could be wholly unsystematic and poorly structured. We foreign medical graduates—FMGs in the jargon of the profession—were, in effect, a medical underclass.

The proportion of FMGs in American hospitals has varied through the years. As of this writing, they are on the wane, and immigration laws that regulate their ingress have become extremely restrictive. But in those years the number was quite high, and in some community hospitals *all* the house staff was composed of foreign doctors. Our work was crucial. FMGs sustained through their effort the enormous health care system of the nation. However, we were often used as cheap labor, in the sense that the amount of time devoted to our instruction was disproportionately small, compared to the many hours we invested in the performance of routine tasks.

All this was accepted with the best of dispositions and in good cheer. We joked among ourselves, without any trace of resentment, saying that we were "intellectual wetbacks," the educated counterpart of the thousands of destitute compatriots who came to take backbreaking jobs in the fields. And it may be that, *toute proportion gardée*, this appraisal was essentially correct. But there was no rancor in any of us. The immigrant expects hurdles along his way. He starts from the proposition that the onus is on him to adjust to a system that predated his arrival; nothing could be farther from his mind than the idea that the system ought to be modified to suit him. The latter is

fundamentally a citizen's notion. Civil disobedience is the luxury of those who already hold a place in civil society and can
find something to disobey. The foreigner has more immediate
and pressing concerns—like, say, survival. He must learn the
language, and the habits and customs of his new neighbors.
And burdensome as his new situation might seem, that from
which he escaped was tougher still.

Moreover, we figured that American society recognizes
diligence, ability, and hard work; that whatever deficiencies and
limitations it may have, arbitrary underestimation of personal
merit is not one of them; and that in a democratic country of
enormous resources and multiple opportunities, the warped,
unfair assessment of one's individual contribution could not
endure for long. Time was to show that in these judgments we
were not mistaken.

However, we were limited in what we could do. The hospital was comparable to those Swiss clinics depicted in novels
of the turn of the century, where the affluent came in search
of a cure for their afflictions amidst pure air and snow-capped
mountain peaks. Such was our work site. Only "consumption"
was no longer prevalent, and the most common diagnosis was
cancer, the hospital having acquired no small renown for ex-
pertise in the treatment of this condition. Here moneyed patients, like their doctors, sometimes seemed to look askance on
us, lowly interns. Nor can it be said that they were entirely to
blame for this attitude. Why, with our unaccustomed look—I
still sported a mustache and longer than customary sideburns
at a time when the clean-shaven look was nearly universal—
ill-fitting uniforms (the only attire I wore for a year, since I
could not afford any other), strong foreign accent, and ignorance of many local ways and hospital routines, we must have
cut sorry and unprepossessing figures. Certain physicians who

cared for the rich saw to it that we were kept away from their patients, unless it was a dire emergency and no one else was available.

Mrs. L—— was one of those patients. During rounds, we were made to understand that we would have no need to enter her private room. The chief oncologist had deputized an advanced trainee, a "fellow," to look after her during late hours, and the rest of the day her room was bustling with regular attending physicians and expert consultants. I was not sorry for being so excluded. Mrs. L—— had the reputation of being a "difficult" patient, the common euphemism for unmanageability and sour temper. Alternatively whining and irascible, now wroth, now querulous, she taxed the patience of the nurses, some of them so saintly that they almost could levitate.

Against all my expectations, I was called to her bedside late one evening. With a look of despair, the nurse in charge informed me that Mrs. L—— demanded to see a physician. The complaint was too trivial, and the hour too late, to summon her private doctor. The "fellow" had been called away by a very serious emergency; and the patient's testiness had proved too much for the night shift. An intravenous drip had to be restarted, and she would not permit anyone to come near her. She demanded to see the house physician. I was assigned to that floor. This time, said the nurse, there was no escape.

Not without trepidation, half asleep from the absurd, grueling hours that we were supposed to keep—a twenty-four-hour on-call period every other day—I appeared at her room's threshold, looking intimidated, disheveled, and even odder than usual. She was a woman in her mid sixties, but she appeared much older on account of her long struggle with cancer. She was propped up with cushions against the back of the bed. An oxygen tube was connected to her nose. Her neck was covered with gauzes and bandages from a recent operation. It seemed incongruous that in her present debilitated condition, she should have managed to create an impression of shrewishness in all who cared for her. However, there was a strangely intense brilliance in her eyes; and her voice, though weakened, had a high-pitched plaintive tone, as of acute distress, which compelled everyone into submitting to her demands. It was as if all that remained of her strength had been concentrated in her gaze and in her voice. These two, she knew, were her last remaining tools with which to manipulate the environment, before sinking to a state of utter dependency.

With a glance that I could not attempt to describe, other than saying that it seemed a hybrid between a scowl and a questioning look, she transfixed me as, accompanied by the nurse, I approached her bed. Before I could do anything, I was severely interrogated: who was I, what was my name, where had I come from, how long had I been there, what did I intend to do, to whom did I answer. And she referred, in a tone of disparagement and execration, to the inept efforts of others, who had preceded me, in setting up the intravenous infusion, and to the suffering their bungling had caused.

Whether she simply needed someone to listen to her, or whether, feeling herself infirm and passive in a world of keen, fit, determined professionals, she was glad to discover someone who looked insecure and in need of encouragement, I cannot say. The fact is, her habitual cantankerousness disappeared. I explained that I needed to do a "cut-down," a skin incision, in order to cannulate a vein. To the amazement of the nurse, and my correspondingly increased prestige on the floor, she acquiesced immediately. I proceeded to dissect a vein of the foot. I was struck by the alabaster whiteness and transparency of her skin, underneath which the blue, branching rills of veins could be seen. The skin was paper thin; I had never seen so fragile and delicate an integument; it could not withstand the mere tightening of sutures without ripping, so that I was forced to approximate the lips of my incision with adhesive tape. Everything I did could have been done more expertly and faster by those whose assistance she had refused. But scarcely did she utter a complaint during my intervention.

It is no small cause of amazement to ponder how little is required, sometimes, to console the distressed. Mrs. L—— clearly had the means to commandeer all sorts of expert professional help. It is equally true that she appeared to be in need of a little humane consideration. For there was no lack of technical competence in her care. Her private doctors daily reviewed the laboratory tests, discussed the X-ray films, wrote the appropriate prescriptions, and carefully monitored the evolution of her disease. But she still expected what those physicians themselves lacked, a bit of human warmth. Not that she wanted someone to hold her hand—this was not her style and might have been too much for her. But a great deal of her anxiety might have dissipated had someone taken ten minutes to talk to her about her present and past life, as I did that night, without deliberate intent to afford relief. Possibly, out of that ever-postponed conversation, her doctors might have heard the question that truly tormented her most grievously; the one question to which all the laboratory tests and all the diagnostic procedures were, in her mind, subservient, yet that no one ever addressed and that she did not find the words to express: "Am I going to die tonight?" Obscure, inchoate, but persistent and ominous, this question lurked in the murky recesses of her consciousness. Ten minutes of sympathetic conversation might have sufficed for Mrs. L—— to formulate it herself, and it would have made a world of difference.

I was neither prepared nor authorized to bring up this vital question. Her end, in fact, was near. She suffered from a rare form of carcinoma of the throat, and all the modalities of conventional therapy had been tried, unsuccessfully. I saw her only two or three times thereafter. Although I had some assignments on her floor, the conspicuous sedulity of nurses, doctors, and technicians, who seemed always to be going in and out of her room, deterred me from stopping by to talk to her in the mornings. I sometimes returned late in the day, only to find her asleep. Yet the rare contacts I had with her were enough for me to find out more facts about her life than many knew who had daily taken care of her. She had been a schoolteacher and had suffered financial need during her youth, in the time of the Great Depression. She married, very young, a merchant who struck it rich: he developed an industrial concern and in time amassed a not inconsiderable fortune. He had died some ten years before she became ill. At his death, she was left a rich widow, without children. She lived alone but was visited often by a niece and an old spinster friend, both her neighbors.

The tumor progressed relentlessly, despite the best efforts of the specialists, to the point of invading the cartilages of the larynx and trachea. For the last few days of her life she could not speak or ingest. It was horrifying to think that if no fatal complication intervened, she would be slowly choked to death, since outside of the local area of involvement the lesions had not been extensive and did not seem to be the chief determinants of her impending demise. The last time I saw her, she was asleep; mercifully, that day she would sink irreversibly into a coma. I remember that there was, on her neck, a tracheostomy orifice (when and why someone had decided to do this, I do not know), and the oxygen tube was now connected to her throat. A very slight fullness of the anterior aspect of the neck was all that could be seen of a lesion that everyone knew had devastated the structures within and would finish by wringing her frail body breathless forever.

As I remember experiences such as this, I cannot avoid thinking that Mrs. L—— died the archetypal death of women in classical Greek tragedy. For to the ancient Greeks the neck was both avatar of Woman's beauty and the site of her maximal vulnerability. For instance, in a Homeric poem to Aphrodite, the goddess is recognized by her superb neck. But it is also by the neck—and strangely, as a scholar has remarked, *by the neck only*—that women are put to death in Greek tragedy, in contrast to the varied ways by which men reach their end.* Thus the same death that lurked in the delicate neck of Iphigenia; the same death that Medea's nurse feared for her mistress—"death by the neck"—throttled the gray-haired former schoolteacher I met in a clinic in the mountains of Colorado.

Her last moments I witnessed almost by accident. I was on her floor and noted some activity in her room. Nurses entered and exited, whispering. I asked the reason for the commotion and was told that she was agonizing; the next of kin were being notified; a priest had come to administer the last rites. I went into the room. It was in semidarkness, except for a small floor light and the outside illumination that came through the window. The gurgling sound of the oxygen flow through the humidifier was all that one could hear; it would soon be turned off. The intravenous solutions had been disconnected: the suspended bottles had dripped empty, and the doctors had ordered that they not be renewed. Mrs. L——

---

* Nicole Loraux, *Façons Tragiques de Tuer une Femme* (Paris: Hachette, 1985).

evinced occasional respiratory movements. Her breathing had become markedly irregular. Rather than breathe, she heaved intermittent sighs, as if her thorax lay wedged between the bed and the resistless crush of a massive weight, allowing her only sporadic, shallow, and rapid inspiratory movements. These ceased at length. Her eyes were fixed and glazed, seemingly frozen while looking at an infinitely distant universe: a world elsewhere; neither here nor there, but past all objective reality. Her jaw suddenly dropped, exposing an edentulous, small, dry mouth. That was all. Her struggle was over.

"She is gone," was the phrase I heard from those present. They uttered it with the assurance of an apodictic truth. And the hearers sent forth the look of intelligence of those who understand. But I did not understand, and to this day I fail to understand what was happening. That she was "gone" could be interpreted literally. Minutes before, there was, on that bed, a blue-eyed querulous former schoolteacher who had known hardships in the Depression, and had loved and married, and had suffered from a harrowing disease. Minutes later, there was, in her place, an unsentient lump of decomposing organic matter. A mannequin. Who brought about this incredible switch? Right under our noses! Look behind the curtains or under the bed: you will find nothing. Where is the person? Vanished. Disappeared. Gone. If it is true that God engineered the miraculous substitution, then our Maker is the supreme prestidigitator and death the unsurpassed magic trick. More amazing even than the fabled rope trick of the Indian fakirs. The number-one sleight of hand for all times.

As to the meaning of the puzzling phrase, I thought I had some inkling of it. Being an immigrant, I began to appreciate what it means to be "gone." To be gone, to have "departed"— terms equally applicable to death and emigration—is essentially to be absent; suppressed as a corporeal presence from the perceptual sphere of others, friend as well as foe. It is to be thought of with melancholy by our loved ones; to be evoked first with painful yearning but later with seething emotions that cool and grow dim, like embers in the midst of ashes. It is to be named first eagerly, then mournfully or solemnly, and at length not at all. To be gone is to be absent, and the absent cannot be seen, except in effigy. But an effigy is an unchanging mask, whereas the reality of the features behind changes, and the features that were before are slowly dissolved in remembrance. For the absent invariably dissolve: theirs is but a ghostly presence, light as the air, which vanishes if one draws near, emitting a phosphorescence before being overtaken by the dark unknown.

I could understand that the émigré and the dead share features in common: *Partir, c'est mourir un peu*—"To leave is to die a little"—says the French proverb. Only where do they go? For both there is another world, an "elsewhere." To the migrant, the new world is in many ways like the old; what migration means to the dead we shall never know. And yet are we not *all* emigrants? For Christianity, the whole of humankind lives in exile, after the forced, vexatious emigration from Paradise, since the Fall. There is also the universal simile, alike Christian and non-Christian, that compares life to a journey and us to pilgrims who grimly endure the trip's vicissitudes before reaching the same, irrevocable destination. Yet, I said to myself, these are *only* metaphors. Poetry. If I wished to understand, to comprehend rationally what the distant look in the eyes of Mrs. L—— signified, I had to search out the answer in concrete, factual knowledge.

Hence I turned to medicine. I asked my mentors what it meant to be gone. "Former, and comparatively more ignorant, generations of medical men," they responded professorially, "believed that if a man stopped breathing and his heart stopped beating, that man could be said to be irretrievably gone—departed for good. Our more enlightened times saw through this fallacy. Today, the highest medical savvy in the land has come up with accurate and reproducible criteria. Besides absent heartbeats and respiration, there must be unresponsiveness to specific stimuli and a certain length of time during which electroencephalographic tracings are reduced to complete flatness."

This answer, however, was unsatisfactory. For the tissues of persons who meet those criteria, when grown artificially in culture media, still manifest all the attributes of life. And their organs, when grafted into a living subject, resume the functions they had before. Now, this conflicts with the idea of "gone forever." For if anything characterizes death, it is absolute finality: death is total, and it is irreversible. It cannot be by bits and pieces. It cannot be temporary. A truly philosophical definition ought to be consistent with this fundamental principle. Therefore, the medical definition that my mentors outlined was intellectually inferior. It was purely a concession to expediency, a way to avoid legal suits and to go on with the various practical businesses of medicine, such as organ procurement for transplants. But this is not the kind of answer I was looking for. I was young, and I hankered after *complete* understanding.

"If what you want is absolute precision and irrefutable truths, do not look to us for that," said my mentors. "We, in medicine, aim to heal the sick. Half of the time we don't know what made a patient sick; the other half of the time we ignore what made the healed recover. We seek the explanations in science. But whether we find them, or no, is secondary to making the sick well. Our job is partly an art and partly a science. Ours is to cure, not to go for certitude."

Therefore, I looked to biological science. It was thrilling for my young mind to realize that death, though uncontemplatable and undefinable, could be defined mathematically, if not verbally. Pharmacology plots dose-effect relationships in neat concave, linear, or sigmoid curves: on one axis, the logarithmic transformation of dosage; on the other axis, the intensity of the effect. And as there is a "median effective dose" (abbreviated ED50), which is the dose of a drug required to produce a specified intensity of effect in 50 percent of the individuals who receive it, just so there is a "median lethal dose," LD50, when the end point is death.

I was fascinated. Was there really such a thing as a "lethal dose"? Death, in my mind, was terminus. I now realized it could be elegantly conceptualized as one point in a series. Alcohol is toxic at a concentration of 1000 mg/L; above 3500 mg/L, it kills. Acetone is injurious at 200 to 300 mg/L; above 550, it is lethal. A drug—alcohol, potassium, or an agent known for its lethal potency—may be ingested without causing death. But only within narrow limits. There is a point at which one more drop, one more milligram, one more milliequivalent, will interrupt the living process. The temperature can be expressed through an infinite number of degrees. Above the extremely hot, as below the incredibly cold, the series may yet be prolonged endlessly. But the living being can exist only within a narrow span of this infinite series: there is a point below which life stops, congealed, another point above which it breaks down by seething. Thus life seemed to me like the crystal wineglass that years ago was used in a television commercial. It sat undisturbed while a singer vocalized in the background. The singer's voice raised its pitch higher and higher, as the camera zoomed in on the wineglass. Then the singer's voice raised its pitch still higher, and the glass shattered. One note below in the register, the glass would hold intact; one note above—the lethal dose—and the glass exploded into fragments.

But this, too, was unsatisfactory. Biological science made broad generalizations. It did not explain individual deaths. The effect of a lethal agent varies with the recipient's age, race or genetic strain, sex, route of administration, and myriad other factors. Two littermates, two identical twins, will react differently to the same dose. There is "individual tolerance" and other imponderables. Scientific concepts of "lethal dose" are expressed as averages of large numbers of experiments but cannot precisely identify or quantitate *individual* liability. And with respect to death, is it not the *individual* that counts? Is it not our own individual deaths that matter most to each one of us?

I imagined that the truth lay in the most precise realm of the sciences: in those scientific heights where conclusions are luminous, irrefutable, and universally valid, as in physics and chemistry. But if I looked into this realm—assuming I could understand what is said in such lofty heights—I was sure to be disappointed. For the higher the reasoning, the less it concerns itself with the individual. Life becomes abstraction. Scientists see life as a precarious—and improbable—equilibrium between the environment and the complex system of macromolecules that constitutes an organism. To maintain this equilibrium requires the input of energy, else the system would naturally tend to disorder, according to the laws of thermodynamics. Death, therefore, is defined as that state in which the energy difference between the macromolecular system and the surrounding environment equals zero.

I confess that the first time I heard propositions of this sort,

I remained speechless. I did not know what to say. That life and death could be defined as mathematically manipulable abstractions seemed to me the zenith of intellectual understanding. But very soon I recovered from the surprise and realized that this answer was as unsatisfactory as the others. For I wanted to know what death means for us as individuals. What use can I make of these abstractions? My death, to me, will mean the end of abstractions, the end of mathematical manipulations, the end of macromolecular equilibrium, the end of thermodynamics. The end of everything.

But perhaps it was not logical understanding that I was after. Perhaps what I needed was that kind of insight which is referred to as "spiritual," not intellectual. The sort of thing mystics speak of and that is said—by those who believe it—to transcend the scope of the reasoning faculty. Nor was I happy with the statements of philosophers and mystics that life must be "a preparation for dying" or "the art of dying." To Montaigne's assurance that a philosophical life consists in learning how to die—*que philosopher c'est apprendre à mourir*—and presumably to die well, I naturally reacted with skepticism about the meaning of the word "learning." Clearly, this is not learning as I understood it. Who can learn *that*? When there are no trials, no rehearsals, no instructors, no teachers, no "quality control," as is now said, no proficiency testing, who can say that he has mastered the "art" of the one experience that is performed once—and once only—and of which no valid reports exist?

But this, of course, is only one of the many contradictions in which we are steeped. From birth to death, the spectacle of our lives is far from tranquilizing. We are born naked, defenseless, insignificant. Despite arrogant pronouncements, despite the high-sounding rhetoric, there is always something pathetic, even contemptible, in our condition. The first part of our lives passes amidst wails and hunger pains, such as are soothed with a little milk. Then we vacillate and totter, and walk on all fours. And all the time, throughout our lives, we remain frail of body, restless of soul, subject to infinite passions, besieged by a multitude of ills, wavering between extremes of joy and sadness. In the bloom of life we are enslaved by our own appetites. At our strongest, the body has the power to oppress us with hunger, to subdue us with sleepiness, burn us with thirst, exhaust us in fasting. But we live on, at once avid and fearful, bored with our possessions but regretful of our losses; conceited with our so-called triumphs in the midst of our miseries. We live on, not knowing what will happen to us, as the hours tick away, each one wounding us, the last one killing us. "*Vulnerant omnes, ultima necat*" was the inscription that Miguel de Unamuno could read on the dial of the clock tower in the central plaza of a Basque little town.

The fact is, in the confrontation between these absurdities, or incomprehensibilities, and the human observer, the result is largely predetermined by the latter's constitution. Human nature is the same, and the most important features of life's experience are common to all. This led Wilhelm Dilthey, German philosopher that he was, to try to systematize in his *Theorie der Weltanschauungen*, all possible visions or ideas regarding life. But even he had to concede that individual temperaments can impart infinite modulations to the same experience. For there are the weak, the nervous, the delicate and morose, who shall dwell in melancholy, fear, and unsatisfaction. And there are also the energetic, the strong, and the sanguine or thick-skinned, who somehow manage to create an armor unto themselves; and covered therewith, they regard the tangle of life by an altogether different light.

When my last hour sounds, one of the latter attitudes should be my only wish: to be blessed with the kind of temper that makes one face life's terminus with any one of a multitude of positive outlooks. I feared vulgarity in life, but for my last moment I would be happy even in vulgarity, if it is good-humored. I could imitate Chrysippus, who died as a result of a violent fit of laughter upon a bad joke: a chronicler says he saw an ass eating his figs and cried out to his wife, "Now give the ass some wine to wash down the figs," and thereupon laughed so heartily that he died. But I should prefer composure, like that of Augustus Caesar, who died with a measured salutation to his wife: "Livia, remember our married life, live, and farewell." Or irony, like that of the emperor Vespasian, who, seized with severe colic and diarrhea, stood up, according to Suetonius, on the premise that an emperor must die on his feet, and cracked one last joke: "Dear me! I must be turning into a god," just before giving up the ghost. Ideally, if I could choose, I would go for the kind of enthusiasm that made Hector Berlioz say in his last moment, to one of his friends: "Now they are *really* going to play my music!"

When my turn comes to emigrate again (this time, I suppose, for what an old professor of mine once referred to as "vertical emigration"), I should wish to bear the experience in the manner of Berlioz: *allegro moderato*, and with hope in the possibility, however unproved and unprovable, that there is a world elsewhere, and with better acoustics.

About the Author

F. González-Crussi was born in Mexico City. He graduated from medical school at the National Autonomous University of Mexico in 1961, obtained postgraduate training in pathology in the United States, and initiated a career in academic medicine at Queen's University in Canada. Returned to the United States in 1973, he managed to combine his love of literature with the practice of pathology, writing both technical, biomedical texts and literary essays. F. González-Crussi is the author of *Notes of an Anatomist, Three Forms of Sudden Death, On the Nature of Things Erotic, The Five Senses, The Day of the Dead,* and *Suspended Animation,* which was named a *New York Times* Notable Book of 1996 and was nominated for the PEN/ Spielvogel-Diamonstein Award for the Art of the Essay. Since 1978 he has lived in Chicago, where he is director of the pathology department of the Children's Memorial Hospital and a professor of pathology at Northwestern University medical school. He is married to Dr. Wei Hsueh, distinguished biomedical researcher, also a pathologist.